DIFFERENT GODS

Different Gods

Integrating Non-Christian Minorities into a Primarily Christian Society

RAYMOND BRETON

McGill-Queen's University Press
Montreal & Kingston • London • Ithaca

© McGill-Queen's University Press 2012

ISBN 978-0-7735-3968-6 (cloth)
ISBN 978-0-7735-3993-8 (paper)
Legal deposit first quarter 2012
Bibliothèque nationale du Québec

Printed in Canada on acid-free paper that is 100% ancient forest free
(100% post-consumer recycled), processed chlorine free

This book has been published with the help of a grant from the
Canadian Federation for the Humanities and Social Sciences, through
the Aid to Scholarly Publications Program, using funds provided by
the Social Sciences and Humanities Research Council of Canada.

McGill-Queen's University Press acknowledges the support of the
Canada Council for the Arts for our publishing program. We also
acknowledge the financial support of the Government of Canada
through the Canada Book Fund for our publishing activities.

Library and Archives Canada Cataloguing in Publication

Breton, Raymond, 1931–

Different gods: integrating non-Christian minorities into a primarily
Christian society / Raymond Breton.

Includes bibliographical references and index.
ISBN 978-0-7735-3968-6 (bound). – ISBN 978-0-7735-3993-8 (pbk.)

1. Religious pluralism – Social aspects – Canada. 2. Religious pluralism –
Social aspects – United States. 3. Religious minorities – Canada – Social
conditions. 4. Religious minorities – United States – Social conditions.
5. Canada – Emigration and immigration – Religious aspects. 6. United
States – Emigration and immigration – Religious aspects. 7. Religion
and culture – Canada. 8. Religion and culture – United States. I. Title.

BL2530.C3B74 2012   200.89'00971   C2011-907183-5

This book was typeset by Interscript in 10/13 Sabon.

Contents

Preface

The last decades have witnessed important changes in the flow of immigrants in the Western world. A substantial proportion of immigrants come from regions of the world that differ from the traditional source countries. Instead of Europe, they come primarily from Southeast Asia, China, the Middle East, Africa, the Caribbean, and Latin America.

In addition, the religious background of a substantial proportion of new immigrants also differs from that of the initial settlers of North America and of the traditional flow of immigrants. Thus for a number of years, immigration has consisted in significant part of non-Europeans and non-Christians coming into a society whose background is basically European and Christian. The changes in the patterns of immigration have generated considerable public debate about the degree and modalities of integration of the new immigrant minorities. Some argue that many fail to adopt the culture and identity of their new society; others claim that their integration into the Canadian and American way of life is progressing normally.

The objective of this book is to present the findings of recent research on religion and the integration of these new cohorts of immigrants, many of whom are non-Christian. The findings that are summarized and analyzed are from the research carried out primarily in North America. Findings from European research are also included at various points of the analysis so as to provide the reader with some benchmarks for the assessment of particular results. The central concern is to analyze the social and cultural processes involved in the integration of immigrants and to identify the factors that facilitate or hinder the process of integration. Although the evidence available does not permit definite conclusions about the pace and degree of integration of the new immigrant minorities into their adopted society, it nevertheless allows the formulation of tentative conclusions in this regard.

The book examines the changes that take place in the religious attitudes and behaviour of immigrants and in the functioning of their religious institutions with time in the host country and especially over generations. Four sets of processes involved in the unfolding of integration are considered. First, what role does religion – as a system of beliefs and moral prescriptions and as a community – play in the transplantation of individuals from one social context to another? Second, is there a progressive dissociation of the properly religious elements of their culture from those that are ethno-cultural and secular? Third, to what extent and in what ways are individual religious attitudes and behaviour transformed with time spent in the new socio-cultural environment? And fourth, how do minority religious organizations change with time?

The analysis also examines the challenges that the incorporation of new immigrant minorities, especially those of different religious backgrounds, brings about for the larger society – for the functioning of its institutions, the definition of the collective identity, and the evolution of its culture. The socio-political and cultural factors that affect the ways in which the processes of incorporation and transformation evolve over time are also considered.

The analysis is not based on data collected specifically for this study. Rather, it is an attempt to integrate into a coherent framework the results of the research literature of the last twenty years or so, with a special but not exclusive focus on the research dealing with the integration of non-Christian immigrant minorities.

The analysis is addressed to students and researchers of ethnicity and immigration. It is also addressed to readers interested in the evolution of our society as a result of this immigration, to those who seek a better understanding of what is involved when someone is transplanted from one social and cultural context to another, and to those who are concerned with the implications of those realities for public policy.

There have been several drafts of the manuscript. Each successive draft was improved as a result of comments from friends and colleagues. For these improvements, I am indebted to Ronald Gillis, Yaacov Glickman, Norbert Hartmann, Ada Jeffrey, Mai Phan, Peter Murphy, and Jeffrey G. Reitz. They generously gave their time to review an earlier version of the manuscript and to offer very helpful comments and suggestions. The comments received from anonymous reviewers were also helpful. I am most grateful to Freya Godard for her competent and thorough editing of the manuscript and to Mai Phan for statistical analyses of data from the Ethnic Diversity Survey.

My deepest gratitude is to my wife, Lily. She encouraged me to pursue this project. Her warm and continuous support over the years made it possible for me to bring it to completion.

DIFFERENT GODS

Introduction

The integration of new immigrants has been a concern in Canada for a significant part of its history. At times, the focus was on settlement in various parts of the country and on economic development. During times of war, the preoccupation was political, driven by fears of disloyalty. The question of integration was seen largely as one of social and political control of certain minorities. In more recent times, with the decline of the birth rate, the emphasis has been on population growth.

The cultural integration of immigrants has always been an important concern because immigrants often differ from the receiving society in some of their cultural characteristics, such as such as language, traditions and customs, and religion. However, when the cultural difference is considered particularly significant, issues of cultural integration acquire a special importance. This appears to be the case recently with the arrival of a significant number of immigrants who are of non-Christian affiliations.

Religion can be the primary context within which personal and social identities are defined. Religion can be an "ethnic-like" marker for newcomers in the sense that it is their religious affiliation that shapes their distinct ethno-cultural identity and the ways in which they are perceived by different groups in the receiving society. Religion may be so important in the social organization of the minority community that the ethnic community can be regarded as a "socio-religious" sub-community (Lewins

1978, 19). In addition, religious organizations can play a role in shaping the relationship of the community and its members to the larger society. In some circumstances, they may maintain a socio-cultural boundary between the minority community and the larger society; under other conditions, they could sustain an antagonistic relation to the larger society. Often, however, minority religious organizations define their role as facilitating the integration of their members into the larger society.

The fact that this change in the religious affiliation of so many immigrants is fairly recent may explain why religion was somewhat neglected for a period of time in social research, at least in comparison to other aspects of the integration of newcomers and their descendants, such as social, economic, and political integration. In Foner and Alba's terms, in earlier research, it has "generally taken a backseat to other topics in the immigration field" (2008, 360).[1] But this relative neglect should not be taken as an indication that religion and religious organizations do not play an important role in the lives of immigrants and members of minorities generally and of their communities. On the contrary, they can assist immigrants in coping with the disruption and loss of control over their lives brought about by being uprooted from one social and cultural world and transplanted into another.

In recent decades, there has been a growing interest in the place of religion in the lives of ethnic communities and their members and its role in their integration into the larger society.[2] Even though the issues pertaining to religion have generally taken a back seat to other topics in the study of immigration, they have not been completely ignored. Indeed, valuable hypotheses for research in this field are provided by scholars such as Mol (1961), Coward and Kawamura (1977), and Mullins (1989) on the transformations in religious organizations and in the practices of individual members as they become progressively integrated into the larger society.

It seems that the increase in interest in those issues in recent decades has been generated by the changing religious demography in several Western countries – a change from primarily Christian to heavily non-Christian immigration in societies that have

Table 1
Religious affiliation in Canada and percentage change, 1991–2001

	Total, 2001	Percentage distribution	Percentage change 1991–2001
Total population	29,639,030	100	9.8
Muslim	579,640	2	128.9
Buddhist	300,345	1	83.8
Hindu	297,200	1	89.3
Sikh	278,410	0.9	88.8
Roman Catholic	12,793,125	43.2	4.8
United Church	2,839,125	9.6	-8.2
Anglican	2,035,500	6.9	-7
Baptist	729,470	2.5	10
Lutheran	606,590	2	-4.7
Presbyterian	409,830	1.4	-35.6
Pentecostal	369,475	1.2	-15.3
Jewish	329,995	1.1	3.7
No religion	4,796,325	16.2	43.9

Source: Statistics Canada 2001.

historically been and in many ways still remain basically Christian. Although non-Christian groups have been present for a long time in Western countries, until recently they were quite small.

Table 1 shows the distribution of the Canadian population for selected religious affiliations and the percentage change from 1991 to 2001. In 2001, Muslims, Buddhists, Hindus, and Sikhs constituted between 1 and 2 per cent of the total Canadian population, but that between 1991 and 2001 all of these religious groups saw considerable growth, from 83 to 129 per cent, depending on the group. In contrast, the total population of the country grew by less than 10 per cent.

The changes in the religious composition of the population have mostly been due to immigration. For instance, before 1961, 85.2 per cent of immigrants to Canada were Christian, compared to 39.6 percent in the period from 1991 to 2001. In contrast, the percentage of immigrants belonging to other world religions increased from 3.8 to 21.5 per cent during that time (Beyer 2005, 176).

FOCUS OF THE STUDY

The central focus of this book is the main processes involved in the integration of members of the ethno-religious minorities, primarily those of a non-Christian background, into the mainstream society. The interaction between newcomers and the established society brings about opportunities and challenges that tend to change with time and especially with generations. This is the case for the immigrants and their communities and for the receiving society. Thus, inevitably, both evolve and change in most areas of life, including the religious.

Each dimension of integration entails its set of processes. The newcomer's integration into the labour market and into political institutions involves somewhat different processes. This so at both the individual and social levels. The integration into social networks and community organizations also entails its distinctive processes, as does cultural integration. The following analysis focuses on one particular component of the culture, namely, religion. What are the particular processes involved in the religious integration of newcomers – especially if their religion is different from that of the majority in the receiving society? How is the life of individuals, of their community organizations, and of the larger society transformed as religious integration takes place? In other words, the book does not consist in a description of the characteristics and experiences of different religious minorities in Canada.[3] Rather its objective is to describe the processes involved in the incorporation of newcomers, their culture, and their institutions into the mainstream society; and some of the conditions or circumstances that may set these processes in motion and under which they unfold. The analysis attempts to pull together the results of several studies carried out in Canada and the United States. It also draws from European research, although the focus is primarily on the ways in which these processes unfold in the Canadian and American social, cultural, and institutional contexts.

Some of the main processes of integration involve the evolution of the attitudes and behaviour of individuals. In addition, some involve the evolution of the religion itself and its traditions, practices, and role in the lives of immigrants, their descendants, and their communities. Some pertain to the relationship between ethno-religious communities and the larger society. The analysis does not address, except tangentially, the role of religion in the maintenance of ethnic identification and culture and their transmission from generation to generation.

Integration is not an event that takes place at one point in time or over a short period. It entails processes that evolve over years and, in many cases, over generations. It is also an interactive and mutual process. That is to say, as newcomers and their descendants become part of the mainstream society, both evolve and change. This takes place in all institutional domains, including the religious. Changes take place in *both* the ethno-religious minorities *and* the mainstream society.

It should also be emphasized that the changes involved in the process of integration are, to a considerable extent, *inevitable* (Hammond and Warner 1993, 56; Kivisto 2007, 56). To some, this may appear to be an inaccurate portrayal of social reality, but, as will be seen, this impression stems largely from a focus on what is happening among new immigrants and also from a focus on failures of integration – which do occur. However, a different picture emerges when what happens over time is taken into account; namely, processes of acculturation and integration into the larger society are set in motion even in the immigrant generation but come to have their full effect with the length of time in the adopted society and in subsequent generations in Canada.

Newcomers and their descendants undergo various kinds of transformations. Individuals change in their religious identities, values, social attachments, and practices. There is an evolution in the role that religion plays in their lives. This tends to be accompanied by changes in their religious commitment and practices. Religious institutions also become more and more different from what they were when first established in Western societies, including Canada. Their doctrines, rituals, behavioural prescriptions, and organizational structures and practices are modified to fit the new circumstances.

Similarly, the identities, social attachments, and values of the individual members of the mainstream society change in response to the growing religious pluralism encountered through interpersonal interaction, through the media, or in different institutional settings. It is not possible for a community that incorporates large numbers of newcomers, especially if they belong to different religious traditions, not itself to be eventually transformed to some degree. The institutions of the society and their agents whose responsibilities bring them into contact with clients, members, and organizational representatives of new religious groups frequently need to modify their rules, practices, and programs – or devise new ones – to respond adequately to new demands.

The identity and culture of the receiving society is one element of the collective life of the receiving society that evolves with the progressive incorporation of new cultural groups and their institutions. The way people think of themselves as a society tends to evolve as more and more people of different backgrounds come to be part of the collectivity. This has occurred in the past. For instance, the prevailing conception of the society and of what was thought to be its central cultural features among English- and French-speaking Canadians was quite different at the beginning of the nineteenth century from what it is today.[4] Many factors have contributed to this evolution, but the changing composition of the population is certainly among them. There is no reason to believe that the society, its identity, and culture will not continue to evolve over time with the continuing change in its socio-cultural composition (as well as in its technological and economic circumstances).

Some transformations take place fairly rapidly while others occur over long periods. The evolution of the processes of incorporation may be fairly easy and harmonious, but it can also be difficult and conflictual. The changes can be experienced as an impoverishment or an enrichment; they can be fairly trouble-free or traumatic. Perceived divergences from or opposition to one's own cultural characteristics may generate tensions in the lives of individual members of minorities and in their kinship and other social relationships. Minority churches and other religious organizations may also find that their ideas, prescriptions, and practices are not quite appropriate in the new social and cultural environment. They experience tensions between the wish to maintain the integrity of the religion and the need to function in a different social, cultural, and legal context.

Similarly, for individuals and institutions of the receiving society, the integration of newcomers, especially if they follow a different religion, may be seen as disruptive of the habitual way of life and organizational practices. The religious beliefs and practices of the newcomers may be perceived as inappropriate. The collective identity of the receiving community – or what it is perceived to be – may be seriously challenged, and significant tensions may be felt between the desire to maintain what is seen as the traditional identity and culture and the requirements of integrating culturally different groups.

Of course, there are variations in the nature and extent of reactions to newcomers in different regions of the country; in communities of different sizes, from metropolitan centres to small towns to rural communities; and in different socio-economic categories, family situations, genders, ages, generations, and lifestyles. Generalizations are difficult, not to say impossible. Rather, there is a multiplicity of patterns. This is the case for religious as well as non-religious attitudes and behaviour.

The progressive integration of newcomers encounters, from time to time, different kinds of difficulties. It may encounter resistance, from segments of the larger society or from the minority itself. The adherents of minority religions may be subjected to negative stereotyping and may experience various forms of social exclusion and hostility, and the resulting social marginalization can seriously hinder the process of integration.

In short, the role of religion is not a static phenomenon in the lives of immigrants and ethnic minorities – or in other components of their lives; nor is it among members of the mainstream society. It evolves over time; the character of their religious experience changes, as does the relationship of individuals with the religious organizations and the other members of their community.

Religion, like ethnicity, can be fundamental in determining the identities of individuals and their socio-emotional bonds. However, neither should be seen as primordial givens of social existence that do not change in the ways in which they play themselves out in the lives of individuals and groups. Ethnicity and religion are realities that can and do change with changing social, economic, political, and cultural circumstances. Their role and importance in shaping the identities and lives of individuals and groups can vary considerably.[5] A "circumstantial" perspective is essential for an understanding of the evolution of minority religious groups and their integration into the mainstream society.

The same can be said about the mainstream society. Its identity, culture, and institutions are not givens of existence that do not (and should not) change with changing circumstances in different domains, such as the economy, technology, communication, and international relations. The increasing presence of people with different religious affiliations and cultural backgrounds constitutes another important component of the changing circumstances. Thus, one set of processes through which religious minorities become part of mainstream society has to do with changes in the mainstream society itself.

Significant increases and changes in immigration bring about ambiguous or undefined situations and social expectations for newcomers and for members of the receiving society. Both are faced with competing systems of meaning and social expectations that may involve a few or several segments of their lives. Such a situation can lead, in both communities, to the emergence of a modified if not an entirely new way of seeing the identity, culture, and historical evolution of their community. It may bring about new approaches to some of its values, norms, customs, and conceptions of what constitutes a well-functioning society and community.

PLAN OF THE BOOK

The book presents an analysis of the processes involved in the integration of immigrants. Following a brief review of the role of religion in the evolution of the journey undertaken by immigrants, the first set of processes examined (in part one) concerns the experience of being uprooted from one social world and transplanted into another. The transplantation experience can entail a cultural disorientation, insecurity about one's identity, and a loss of control over one's life. Transplantation also entails establishing roots in the society of adoption – a process that may meet some resistance and even opposition. Newcomers and minorities in general may find that some members of the established community maintain a social distance from them. In more extreme cases, what takes place is rejection and even outright hostility.

Soon after immigrating, other challenges are felt by members of minorities with regard to their religious identity, beliefs, normative prescriptions, and practices (see part two). The cultural dilemma entails uncertainty and a questioning of the religious heritage, an experience that can generate a certain degree of anxiety. One area of questioning has to do with which elements of the culture are properly religious and which derive from their ethnic or national background. Life in a different cultural milieu can lead to a dissociation of religion from ethnicity.

The established systems of meanings, doctrines, rituals, symbols, and practices lose some of their relevance or applicability in the new social context. Religion may decline as a basis of social identity and community attachments. Individuals may abandon their religion altogether or some features of the traditional religious culture and practices. But another response to the lack of fit between the traditional religion and the cultural context is possible, namely to adapt the religion creatively to the new context.

Communal religious institutions also face a challenge (see part three). Leaders come to see a lack of fit between their traditions and the new cultural milieu. That is to say, it is not only individuals that undergo processes of acculturation; minority religious institutions are also progressively transformed in the process of attempting to meet the needs of their members in the new social circumstances. An important response to these changes is to shift the focus of organizational activities from immigrant adaptation to what could facilitate the full participation of their members in the host society.

Another response is to creatively modify the properly religious dimension of the religion and its organizational embodiment. Doctrines are reinterpreted in such a way as to make sense in the new cultural environment. Similarly, normative prescriptions and liturgical practices are modified in response to new circumstances. In the process, confrontations, debates, and negotiations may take place among subgroups in the congregation over the proper interpretations of the doctrine and its moral prescriptions or over rituals and practices.

Members of the mainstream society also face some challenges, especially if the minorities adhere to religions different from their own (see part four). But immigrants may also bring with them varieties of Christianity (for example, various denominations and sects) that can be quite different from the ones or ones prevailing in the receiving society.

The incorporation of minorities is not only a matter of individual integration. It also involves the institutional recognition of the new religion. Institutions are pressured to respond to the needs and demands of newcomers. Thus, the process also entails the incorporation of minority religious institutions into the cultural and institutional fabric of the larger society. This usually involves some changes in the character and practices of institutions and their organizational components. The more culturally different the newcomers, the greater the challenges are likely to be for the host society.

The following analysis is based primarily on the research literature of the past twenty years or so (with some exceptions),[6] a limitation that does not, however, apply to the theoretical literature. Not surprisingly, given the demographic trends noted above, much of the research during this period deals with situations where the minority religion is different from that of the mainstream society. It also draws primarily from the North American literature. However, some research carried out in the United Kingdom and Europe is included because it confirms, spells out further, or illustrates some of the patterns and processes of integration identified in the analysis or some of the factors that may trigger social processes that result in particular patterns of integration or failures of integration. Although an attempt has been made to include as much of the relevant research as possible, there is certainly no pretence that the analysis is exhaustive.

PART ONE

Religion and Religious Organizations and the Transplantation Experience

Immigration is an experience of being uprooted from one social world and transplanted into another. It entails having to deal with uncertainty and the risk of not being able to rebuild a satisfactory life in the new socio-cultural environment. Many of the situations that immigrants face are quite different from those they learned to cope with in their country of origin. Besides meeting basic survival needs, they face a culture with unfamiliar conceptions of social, economic, political, and religious realities. They have to deal with various institutions that embody those conceptions in their rules and practices.

The challenges of social transplantation tend to lead to the formation of community organizations. New immigrants form associations for mutual support, to exchange information, or simply not to feel lost in the new environment. The sense of a common identity and the desire to keep alive the cultural, including religious, traditions can also lead to in-group social relations. The solidarity that develops among people in such a situation is based primarily, but not exclusively, on the requirements of adjusting to the new environment. It may be referred to as *adaptive solidarity*. Of course, issues of adaptation may remain beyond the first generation, but they are especially salient for the immigrant generation.

The transplantation metaphor can be extended to include the idea that it may trigger rejection mechanisms in the receiving "body." The simple presence of "outsiders" may lead to a sense of superiority among some members of the established community, together with a reluctance to accept "others" into their community (Elias and Scotson 1994). Being categorized as "other" establishes a social distance between categories of people. In other words, immigrants and their descendants may experience various modes of social marginality.

I

Cultural and Social Transplantation

Religion and religious organizations can play a critical role in helping immigrants to cope with the difficulties and challenges of transplantation. Hirschman (2004, 1228) summarized the centrality of religion to immigrant communities as the search for refuge, respectability, and resources: refuge from the trauma of loss and separation, respectability in the attainment of a certain social status, and resources for survival and effective functioning in a new social environment.

Religion can be seen as having a threefold role in the process of adaptation.[1] First, a religious anchorage can assist individuals in coping with the cultural disorientation and the accompanying need to redefine their social identity that is brought about by the immersion in a new cultural environment. Second, churches can assist immigrants in coping with the possible disruption of their social networks and loss of social status that may have resulted from the social and cultural transplantation. Third, churches and other religious organizations can help immigrants deal with social marginality.[2]

CULTURAL DISORIENTATION AND IDENTITY CHALLENGES

Transplantation necessarily entails a discontinuity in social life and a disorientation generated by the encounter with different social expectations. The cultural change is likely to be experienced as a cultural loss. The period of transition can be more or less prolonged. It will occur even if the migration is voluntary, but it is likely to be more pronounced among refugees and involuntarily displaced persons.

For most immigrants, the transplantation involves a shift from being part of a majority in their country of origin to being part of a minority. Being born in a minority situation has its challenges, but becoming a member of a minority as a new experience can, in itself, be somewhat disorienting. Immigrants may know in advance that this will happen, but having to live the change is another matter.

The experience of cultural discontinuity and disorientation tends to be accompanied by an intensification of the human need for meaning (Salzman and Halloran 2004). Continuity is a central dimension of identity; it involves "the feeling that ... what one is doing, thinking, and feeling now is meaningfully related to what has gone before and to what will come later (Hewitt 1989, 153)."

Continuity is the sense of being the same person as external circumstances change. Religion can provide that continuity for many individuals. It can be or become a source of meaning. The experience of transplantation can result in an intensification of the religious commitment because it provides a spiritual orientation that counters the confusion created by the challenges of a life in a new and demanding culture (Smith 1978, 1174ff.).[3]

Berger (1967, 22) points out that the experience of being separated from the society into which one was integrated and being submerged in a social world that is different and poorly understood and whose members' expectations can be confused and confusing exposes individuals to dangers and challenges they cannot cope with by themselves – the ultimate danger being meaninglessness (see also Driedger 1980). Given such a discontinuity in one's socio-cultural experience and such uncertainties in one's life, religion with its beliefs, values, rituals, and communal encounters can be a source of meaning. It can provide immigrants

with spiritual therapy, insight into their transplantation experience, and hope for the reconstruction of their lives. Religion can
be important in relation to the "psychic" cost of the transition
from one society to another. It has been noted, for example, that
a number of Canadian Muslim immigrants have turned to Sufism
– a spiritual tradition in Islam – to find spiritual resources that
can counter the confusion created by the challenges of a life in a
new and demanding social world (McDonough and Hoodfar
2005, 133).

In other words, religion can provide *symbolic resources* to individuals as they go through the experience of being uprooted
and transplanted into a new social environment. Such resources
consist in a system of meanings or interpretive schemes, a normative framework, and an identity based on shared beliefs and
cultural values through which the experience of transplantation
is interpreted (Hirschman 2004, 1207, 1210, 1224–6). Culture,
including religious culture, provides publicly available symbolic
forms through which people experience and express meaning.

Swidler (1986, 277–8) suggests that culture can be seen as a
"tool kit" of symbols, stories, rituals, world views, and ways of
life that people can use in varying configurations to solve different kinds of problems. In settled lives, culture and its values and
norms are integrated with action. In unsettled lives, which in
varying degrees are the lives led by immigrants, individuals lose
their firm rooting in the tradition in which they have been socialized. The role of culture then is not so much to sustain existing
strategies of action as to devise new ones. The responses to inter-
views with young British Pakistanis indicate that Islam does provide them with such a tool kit, that is, symbolic resources for
dealing with the ambiguities and contradictions that they experience in their new social environment (Jacobson 1997, 253–4).

A self-defining ideology may exist in a cultural group
(Vertovec 1990, 240). Such an ideology is self-defining because
it involves a reflection on features of the group's distinctiveness
based on observations concerning the group's past, present, and
future collective experience. This may include the production of

somewhat new historical narratives, the "invention" of tradition, and the "symbolic construction" of the "community" in the process of formation.[4]

When religious beliefs are part of or constitute its core, the ideology is a symbolic resource that can have an especially pervasive intellectual and affective power since it is believed to "carry and bestow an authority perceived as emanating from a transcendent source." Thus, religion can provide an otherworldly rationale for immigrants' pursuits. Otherworldly religious transcendence can be related dialectically to the motivation, discipline, and courage needed for this-worldly social and political action (Vertovec 1990, 226–7).

THE DISRUPTION OF SOCIAL LIFE

Newcomers are strangers in the new social setting and, as such, are likely to experience a disruption in their social networks and a loss of social status. They have to reconstruct their social worlds, build new social networks, acquire an adequate social standing in the community, find their way in the economic and social institutions in which they are now pursuing their lives, and learn to deal with governmental and other agencies. In short, they face the challenge of fitting in while maintaining their cultural and personal integrity (Warner and Wittner 1998, 37).

Because of the newness of the circumstances and the complexity of the task of reconstructing their lives in a new cultural and economic environment, newcomers tend to have a relatively low sense of control over the rebuilding of their lives. Of course, since individuals differ in the resources at their disposal, such as education, financial resources, or access to a cohesive kinship network and friendship ties, considerable variations can be expected in the degree of control they have or feel they have over their life trajectory.

In addition, features of the international context – wars, revolutions, and terrorism – at the time of immigration may be such as to reduce further their sense of control over their lives. For instance, because of contemporary conflicts and their historical background, Muslims in a Western country may be less masters of their own destiny than individuals of other religious backgrounds, particularly those of the same religious background as the host population (Cesari 2004a, 21–2). That can also be the situation of immigrants or members of minorities whose ancestry is in a region with which the host country is in conflict or at war; (that would have been the case for Japanese and Germans in an earlier period). It can also be the situation if the immigrant is from a country that at one time was a colony of the receiving society.

Important events in the local, national, or international scenes may become associated in the public's mind with particular groups. These events come to shape the perceptions of what is distinctive of the groups and as a result can become the critical elements of social differentiation. They become the basis for the definition of social boundaries. Recently, events such as September 11 and other instances of terrorism in different parts of the world have increased the social and political salience of religion, especially Islam – and largely in a negative way. In such circumstances, the social integration of newcomers is not so much under their own control as under the influence of external circumstances. They experience a loss of control over the definition of their social identity.

A related circumstance that may result in a loss of control over the definition of their social identity occurs when immigrants see themselves as nationals from another country but are instead defined by members of the receiving society as members of a religious group, such as Muslims, Hindus, or Sikhs (Naguib 2002, 161).

Churches and other religious organizations can also provide *social resources* to members of ethnic minorities.[5] Through the religious community, individuals involved in the same experience of transplantation and adaptation may gain mutual understanding and encourage each other. They can also assist each other with economic problems, cultural enigmas, hostility or discrimination, and governmental and other bureaucracies.

This support can occur at all stages of the transplantation and integration process. As described by Hagan and Ebaugh (2003,

1154), it may be available in connection with the decision to migrate in the form of information and guidance, as well as legitimacy for the decision through counselling. In the preparation for the journey, religious organizations can help with travel arrangements. There may also be of assistance on the journey itself as when a pastor tries to reach the migrant's relatives in the country of destination or, in the case of migrants who have been detained by the authorities at border checkpoints, to solicit help from someone who has contacts with the legal system. The role of religious organizations extends also to the process of arrival and settlement in the new country.

On the place of religious organizations among Sikhs, O'Connell (2000, 198) notes that "in a very basic sense, the *gurdwara* is a meeting place, a physical place with psychic space for greeting friends (an especially valuable function for recent immigrant women, who otherwise might have little scope for socializing beyond the home). It is a place for making useful business, social and, political contacts and for bringing together Sikh playmates for children and Sikh friends (and prospective spouses) for Sikh youth ... It is also a place for mobilizing the congregation to face problems and opportunities affecting the community at large." Nayar (2004, 142) also observed that most of the interviewees participating in the study described going to the *gurdwara* for social activities rather than for prayer or for learning about the religion.

The social resources provided can increase the control immigrants have over their life circumstances. Immigrants tend to "make more use of, or rely more strongly on, religion when they feel little control over the situation they confront; when risks are extremely high" (Hagan and Ebaugh 2003, 1159). The low sense of control may be the result of having to cope with situations and events in the receiving society. However, it may also result from situations in their own cultural group, as in the feeling of a loss of control by parents over their children, or men over women, especially their wives. Religion may then be brought into play to maintain or re-establish traditional relations that are threatened in the new cultural environment.[6]

One of the main kind of support provided by religious organizations is a sense of belonging. Such a sense offers individuals an anchorage for their personal identity and self-esteem. Because of this, religion can be a critical factor in their psychological well-being. In addition, being socially integrated is a resource that individuals can use in the pursuit of personal and social goals. It is a resource in the sense that social integration entails socio-emotional support, social approval, contacts, and valuable information. Such support is so basic that it is a social expectation that comes automatically with being a member of a group, community, or society. Indeed, the opposite is estrangement, a feeling akin to that of being a stranger.

One reason why religious organizations play such a significant role is that they combine symbolic, social, and sometimes material resources. For that reason, they can be a source of empowerment that can be quite significant for immigrants dealing with the experience of uprooting and transplantation (Warner, 1993, 1068–9).

Of course, not all immigrants and members of minorities may draw both types of resources from religion and religious organizations. A study of Muslim Arab immigrants revealed two types of community organization among the respondents, one based on personal networks of family and friends and another based on organizations. For those whose community is of the first type, the practice of religion is not dependent on mosque attendance; rather, it is a private matter. It could be said that religion provides them with symbolic resources. This appears to be the prevailing pattern among women who see their role as safeguarding the culture and protecting the young from negative American influences (Lin 2009, 282, 284).

For those whose networks are largely (but not exclusively) within organizational settings, the mosque is not only a place of worship. It is also a community centre for a variety of social, political, and professional purposes. Religious organizations provide access to social resources. This seems to be the case mostly (but not exclusively) for men of relatively high socio-economic status. The patterns may also be different for first and subsequent generations. In short, this research underscores the importance of assessing, not only the role of Islam in the process of adaptation, but also the role played by whatever Muslim community is important for various categories of individuals (Lin 2009, 279, 287).[7]

COLLECTIVE AS WELL AS INDIVIDUAL INTEGRATION

Immigrants have to fit in as individuals but also as a distinct collectivity. They need to gain social acceptance as members of a group who identify themselves and are identified by others as different. Thus, the challenge is not only their own individual social standing in the society but also that of their group. Accordingly, they are likely to "experience the need to define themselves as a group for a variety of purposes ranging from the articulation of identity as a conscious value for its own sake to its importance as a means of attaining political power, group mobilization and/or resistance and, more commonly, to stave off the (perceived) threat of assimilation" (Winland 1993, 115; Kahani-Hopkins and Nick Hopkins 2002).

In this collective regard, churches and religious organizations can play a significant role. A group's self-defining ideology (noted above) can provide the rationale for programmatic calls for action, and it is an integral part of the process of ethnic mobilization. It is also through this ideology that members of the group place themselves vis-à-vis other groups and societal institutions (Vertovec 1990, 240).

Churches and religious organizations can also provide an organizational base for collective action through leadership – either that of clergy or laity – that financially is largely independent of the larger society and that is skilled in managing people and resources. They constitute an organizational apparatus for the mobilization of labour and material resources, and for the organization of social or political action aimed at fighting discrimination, gaining recognition from the public and societal institutions, and obtaining services for their members. In short, they can provide a basis of collective empowerment for social change.

As suggested by Lin (2009), an empirical question is the relative importance of symbolic and social resources for immigrants in coping with the transplantation experience. Connor's study also underscores this research need. In his analysis of a Canada-wide sample of immigrants, he observed a decline, with time in Canada, in church or temple attendance but an increase of religious volunteering. (See chapter 4 for a further discussion of Connor's findings.) This suggests that the communal dimension of church membership becomes more important over time while the symbolic dimension decreases marginally. On the other hand, the relative importance of these two dimensions of church membership may depend on the family, social, and economic circumstances of immigrants and on the social context in which they are pursuing their integration experience. Some relevant research findings are reviewed in a later chapters (see part three), but additional research on this matter is definitely needed.

There may also be significant variations among individuals in the extent to which religion affects the process of coping with the various challenges of transplantation. There are no doubt individual and subgroup variations in the ways in which newcomers evaluate and apply the values and norms of their religion – if they do so at all. Religious affiliation and practice are important for an understanding of the strategies adopted in the process of adaptation; but variations in religious concepts and orientations within a particular religious tradition would also seem to have explanatory potential.

A variation that may be of significance is the individual's concept of God. Maynard et al. (2001, 67) identified several ways in which people described their concepts of God: benevolent, wrathful, omnipotent, guiding, false, stable, deistic, worthless, powerful, condemning, and caring. Their research observed a correlation between the concepts of God held by respondents and their inclination toward one of four religious coping styles. For example, those who see God as benevolent and guiding are more likely to favour the "surrender style in which the individual works with God while valuing God's direction above his or her own." On the other hand, a positive correlation was observed between a view of God as false (a non-entity), deistic (distant) or worthless (removed from human affairs) and "the Self-directing style in which an individual takes an active problem-solving stance and does not involve God directly" (2001, 72).[8]

The direction of the relationship between concept of God and coping style also requires empirical examination. Does an individual's concept of God affect the formulation of strategies of action, or is the concept a conclusion reached after one's strategies are seen as having either succeeded or failed?

CONCLUSION

The experience of being uprooted from one social world and transplanted into another usually involves some degree of cultural disorientation, identity insecurity, and loss of control over one's life circumstances. Religion can assist newcomers in coping with such experiences. Indeed, religion and religious organizations can provide *symbolic* resources that immigrants can draw upon: a system of values and meanings and a normative framework that can provide a cultural and psychological anchorage for individuals and families. But people can also find *social* assistance in the religious organizations of their community. To a significant extent, religious organizations are communal organizations and not only places of worship. In fact, for many, they may be more important as centres of social encounters and cultural activities than as sites for religious services. However, as noted, there may be significant variations among individuals and subgroups in the extent to which religion plays a role in the process, in the ways in which it operates in their lives, and whether it is the symbolic, the social, or both dimensions of religion that matter.

Social marginality can also be part of the experience of being uprooted from one social world and transplanted into another. It may result from different social processes and is likely to have an impact on individuals and on their relations to the larger society and its institutions. Religion and religious organizations can help individuals to deal with such experiences. This is discussed in the following chapter.

2

Religion and Social Marginality

Immigrants and their descendants can become socially marginal as a result of different kinds of social processes. The social distance between them and the larger receiving society may be moderate or pronounced: it may vary from being unaccepted or treated differently because the newcomers are different from the larger society to outright social and economic exclusion.

THE EXPERIENCE OF SOCIAL DISTANCE OR REJECTION

Perhaps the most benign manifestation of the reluctance to accept newcomers consists in pressure on members of the minority to conform and to relinquish their background. This is especially the case if the minority religious culture is considered inferior or backward. Pressures to conform may include two opposite social forces: they can be at the same time towards inclusion through rapid acculturation and social differentiation through categorization by an emphasis on their differences from the majority.

More threatening and difficult are the experiences of discrimination, social exclusion, and social aggression (verbal or physical). Such negative experiences may or may not co-exist with pressures to assimilate, even though the two attitudes are contradictory: one cannot simultaneously expect the social inclusion and exclusion of a category of people. Frequently, those who are accused of being clannish and unwilling to assimilate are those who are the most likely to experience various forms of social exclusion. Their so-called clannishness is, in part, a response to the non-acceptance as equals.

The notion of citizenship assumes that members of a nation have certain common features, such as origin, culture, religion, and so on. "The imagined commonality, and the distinction from others inherent in it, is expressed in the notion of citizenship, a formalized criterion for the distinction between 'full members' and 'foreigners'... If they are regarded primarily as foreigners, they have *de jure* an inferior position in law, and can consequently make less claim on social goods and services" (Rath et al. 2001, 17). This would also be the case if there is a public perception of foreignness without *de jure* force.

Such an experience can happen to immigrants when they are not considered to be fully Canadian, a view that exists in certain segments of the population. A survey carried out in 1997 found that about three out of ten Canadians think that "immigrants cannot expect to be considered as fully Canadian as those who were born and raised here." It should be noted that "Canadian" is a denotation that includes not only the "old-stock Canadians" but also the minorities whose religious symbols and practices are the same as those of the mainstream society (Breton et al. 2004, 64).

That feeling can also be instilled into members of minorities by a public discourse that includes distinctions between those who and those who are not; and between those who have their cultural roots here (who are "de souche") and those who do not. The same thing can happen to non-whites who are asked what country they come from though their families have been in Canada for generations, to those whose culture is denigrated, and to those who do not speak the language of the majority or speak it with an accent that is different from that of the majority.

In recent years, the mainstream society has seemed to focus increasingly on religion rather than on ethnicity – although in a number of cases, different bases of identification are closely related in the public mind. There are a number of reasons for this. For instance, as noted earlier, a characteristic of the "new" immigration is that a large proportion of newcomers are of non-European, non-Christian origins, who are coming into a society that is largely of European and Christian background (Gans 1994, 589). This is not to suggest that marginalization and exclusion have been the experience only of religious groups outside the Christian tradition. Historically, Catholics and minority Protestant groups have been subjected to prejudice, discrimination, and social marginalization.

But it is not only differences in religion that matter. There is also the fact that religious membership may be intertwined with ethnic or racial identity. Data from the Ethnic Diversity Survey (carried out in 2002 across Canada) show a close connection between ethno-racial background and religion: Christians are primarily of European or white origins; the same is true of Jews. Among the other religious groups, Muslims and Buddhists are the most diverse in their origins. About half of Buddhists are Chinese, nearly 30 per cent are Southeast Asian; the rest have a variety of other origins. Muslims are divided into two major groups: about 38 per cent are Pakistanis or Indians of East African background; 45 per cent are Arab and West Asian (most of whom classify themselves as visible minorities but some as white). Another 8 per cent are Black. By contrast, Hindus and Sikhs are more homogeneous in terms of origins, both groups being almost exclusively of South Asian origin (Reitz, Banerjee, et al. 2009).

In addition, events on the international scene have also influenced the public perceptions of particular religions. In fact, Nielsen (1991, 49) suggested that the negative "perceptions of Islam and Muslims in the wider European society have been determined much more by international political events than by the settled Muslim communities themselves." When threatening events are perceived to have been brought about by members of particular cultural, religious, or racial groups, the result is usually social polarization and conflict. Specifically, responses to heightened fears, anxiety, and efforts at self-protection tend to target members of a particular out-group who are seen as responsible for the events – Muslims in the current international context. Such feelings also lead people to identify more strongly with their own group (Blumer 1958). There is an increased emphasis on the distinct identity of each group and an accentuation of their differences. In threatening situations people become more accepting of those who are similar to themselves and more hostile toward those who are different. In other words, inter-group tensions involve an increase in the *salience of group identities and inter-group boundaries*. In recent times, it appears that those boundaries are more likely to be religious than ethnic.

What differentiates the polarized groups is likely to become more salient because the dynamic of conflict entails a tendency to generalize the attitudes and behaviour of particular individuals to the entire group. It is "us" against "them." The other group progressively ceases to be seen as consisting of different individuals and comes to be seen as a single entity homogeneous in its opinions, attitudes, and culture and in its designs in relation to the community or society in which it finds itself.[1]

The perceptions and categorizations that progressively emerge can become broadly accepted by the media and the public at large and ultimately by the immigrants themselves (Sarna 1978, 372). The categorizations of Islam (and of peoples stereotypically all seen as Muslims, such as Arabs) in the Western media has been largely negative. Much of the coverage has been one-sided and sensationalist. It has the effect of confirming rather than questioning our old inherited Christian-Western stereotypes and prejudices about Islam and Muslims (Sander 1991, 62). A study of over nine hundred Hollywood films revealed that moviegoers would be led to believe that all Arabs are Muslims and that all Muslims are Arabs. In addition, they are portrayed as "heartless, brutal, uncivilized, religious fanatics" (Shaheen 2003, 171).

Images and ideas about religious minorities can also be shaped by textbooks. A study of the coverage of Islam and Muslims in twenty-one French-language high-school textbooks used in Quebec in 2003–4 revealed positive developments in the sense that the openly negative attitudes toward Islam and Muslims found in 1980s textbooks have by and large disappeared. However, the study also showed that there is still a significant amount of ethnocentric and stereotypical presentations, as well as factual errors (McAndrew et al. 2007).

Eid's research in Montreal shows that a strong majority of young Arab-Canadian youth are under the impression that Canadians portray Arabs in a stereotypical and prejudicial manner. These attitudes are not linked to events in the Middle East, but rather to Hollywood movies, which are seen "as the most important catalyst for the production of anti-Arab and anti-Muslim prejudices" (Eid 2007, 186). (It should be noted that the data for this study were collected before September 11.)

Other survey results paint a more positive picture. For example, in a poll in 2007, 75 per cent of Canadian Muslims said that "just some or very few" of their fellow citizens are hostile to Muslims and only 17 per cent indicated "most or many" – this latter percentage being much lower than in Britain (51 per cent), Germany (39 per cent), France (33 per cent) and Spain (31 per cent) according to polls conducted by the Pew Research Center (Reitz, Banerjee, et al. 2009, 697).

A review of the various forms of discrimination experienced by Muslims in Canada in the weeks that followed the terrorist acts in the United States in September 2001 revealed an increase in hate crimes (mostly in the form of insults), ethnic profiling by the police and intelligence authorities, negative news coverage, and negative attitudes among 30 to 45 per cent of the Canadian population. These expressions of suspicion and hostility towards the Muslim population appeared to reduce their access to labour-market opportunities. These manifestations of suspicion and hostility subsided in the following years (Helly 2004).

A recent survey among a sample of Canadians[2] of attitudes vis-à-vis religious groups revealed that "many Canadians harbour deeply troubling biases" (Geddes 2009, 20).[3] It showed, for instance, that while only 10 per cent said they thought Christianity teaches violence, 45 per cent said they believe Islam does, and 26 per cent saw Sikhism as encouraging violence. Such views may have been shaped, in part, by international and local events and their media coverage (21).

The survey showed that 83 per cent would accept their child marrying a Christian, 56 per cent a Jew, 53 per cent a Buddhist, 46 per cent a Hindu, 39 per cent a Muslim, and 39 per cent a Sikh (Geddes 2009, 23). However, it also revealed that respondents were more likely to approve of one of their children marrying a follower of a given religion than to view that religion favourably. This underscores the importance of distinguishing interpersonal attitudes from the "sense of group position." The latter has to do with perceived *group* competition and conflict. While the former concerns specific individuals, the latter refers to the perceived political, economic, or cultural threats that other groups represent for one's own group (Blumer 1958; Bobo and Hutchings 1996, 952). So, one can be negative vis-à-vis a group but not vis-à-vis particular individuals (this is the "some of my best friends are ..." phenomenon).

The sense of group position in relations between immigrant and native groups may involve an increase in the salience of a particular social characteristic – religious, in this case – as an object of identification and as a basis for the definition of personal and social identities. This increase may take place through processes of "reactive identity formation" (Cesari 2004a, 25). That is, pressures to assimilate, social exclusion, and negative stereotyping tend to reinforce the minority-group identification and social attachments within their own group. Encountering barriers to full participation in the larger society, including in mainstream churches, may be a strong incentive to form and maintain a distinctive community. These experiences constitute the basis of a defensive solidarity. "The process of forging a *reactive ethnicity* (or religion) in the face of perceived threats, persecution, discrimination and exclusion is not uncommon. It is one mode of ethnic identity formation, highlighting the role of a hostile context of reception in accounting for the rise rather than the erosion of ethnicity (or religion)" (Rumbaut 2008, 3; see also Cadge and Davidman 2006, 33, and Chong 1998, 268).

Nielsen (1991, 49) notes that the effect of hostile public opinion in Europe "has consistently been to limit the space in which Muslim organizations can constructively manoeuvre, and some have adopted the only other alternative, namely aggressive self-assertion." This is related to the low degree of control discussed above.

Such reactive processes may perhaps be more likely if a religious rather than an ethnic identification is salient in a particular societal context. That is, it can be argued that, generally, individuals will relinquish ethno-cultural elements of their background more easily than their religious beliefs and practices. If to conform means abandoning one's religion, for many it will act as a pressure to reaffirm their religious commitment. As put recently by a Muslim in Europe: "If becoming European means abandoning one's religion, many will choose not to be European" (quoted in the *Toronto Star*, December 30, 2006).

In this regard it is important to distinguish between the perceptions of members of minority groups of their own personal experiences and that of the community to which they belong. In his study of second-generation Arabs in Montreal, Eid (2007, 187) found that a large majority of his Montreal Arab youth respondents felt personally accepted by their fellow Canadians even though, as noted above, the majority also felt that Canadians portrayed Arab Muslims in a stereotypical and prejudicial manner (Eid 2007, 187). In other words, it may be that the perceived attitudes toward the group matter more than one's personal inter-group experience.

RELIGION AND COPING WITH SOCIAL MARGINALITY

Religion and the religious community can play an important role in assisting members of minorities who experience a failure of social integration because of non-receptive and even hostile attitudes on the part of members of the receiving society. Social marginality in the sense of feeling unattached to both the ethnic community and the larger society could also be a manifestation of the failure of integration and could lead to a sense of alienation. Such experiences can produce a variety of responses on the part of immigrants and members of minorities generally. In the case of minority religious groups, they may increase the salience of their religion over their ethnicity. They may also lead to the adoption of a defensive strategy, such as retreating socially within the protective boundaries of their own ethno-religious community with its distinctive beliefs and customs. This tends to reinforce social boundaries and slow the process of acculturation (Kivisto 2007, 504–5).

An Increase in the Salience of Religion, Subjectively and as a Social "Marker"

The experience of being different that such a situation generates may increase the salience of a person's own religion. This is the case, for example, with Muslims who immigrate to a country in which Christianity has been and continues to be the dominant religious tradition. In Islam, for example, the emphasis is on rightful action, which means that to be a devout Muslim one must behave in certain, explicitly defined ways. A Muslim is morally obliged to do so by his belonging to the Muslim community. The differences that distinguish observant Muslims from non-Muslims tend to be demonstrated in normal interaction and continually, rather than merely from time to time. In contrast, there are few, if any, practices that Christians (at least in the Western world) need to demonstrate in day-to-day interaction in order to see themselves and be seen as observant Christians (Jacobson 1997, 247–8).

Such minority-mainstream differences and historical experiences involving religion may increase the salience of religion over ethnicity and race as a social "marker" of social identification. The visibility of religious symbols and practices or those that are closely associated with a particular religion may focus the attention of outsiders on religious markers. Sometimes, however, it is "thrust upon one without regard to their religious practices or lack thereof. Several respondents used the long and bitter history of anti-Semitism to explain why they were educating their children to be aware that they are Jews – 'because if I don't tell them, someone else may, and under terrible circumstances'" (Cadge and Davidman 2006, 33).

Not only may the salience of religion increase under the influence of external circumstances, but it may also be the outcome of strategies used by individuals in social encounters. It is possible that among non-whites, for instance, a religious identification is preferable to a racial one. The choice of religious identification may be made to avoid having to confront their racial location in the society. "For a group which is defined as being both different and inferior and denied opportunities to assume identity and status relevant to the mainstream of the metropolitan society, self-conception and self-esteem may increasingly focus on religious beliefs and practices and its reconstruction in a less friendly and even an 'alien milieu'" (Barot 1993, 8).

The failure of integration has led a number of Black Americans to convert to Islam. "Avoiding the stigma attached to segregation requires dissociating from the dominant culture as far as possible ... [and] conversion to Islam seems a viable way to transform racial stigma from a liability to an asset" (Cesari, 2004a, 25). A similar phenomenon has been noted among the young of Maghreb or Black African origin in France. The ostentatious character of Islam among them is a reaction to a stigmatization based on their origin, their accent, and the colour of their skin. It is an attempt to assume and assert a different Islamic identity, which is a voluntarily chosen positive identity in place of the negative one imposed by others (Khosrokhavar, 1997, 41).

Ethnicity and religion may be inherited through early socialization in a family rooted in a particular group. But, as noted earlier, this does not mean that such cultural traits and social attachments are fixed for life. On the contrary, they can and do change as individuals move from one social context to another or as they encounter new circumstances. Individuals are not passive recipients of identities and cultural attributes but active agents in their construction. Ethnic and religious identities and identifying markers can be seen as acquired features of identity, available for use by participants in an encounter and subject to presentation, inhibition, manipulation, and exploitation so as to maximize the benefits of the encounter (Lyman and Douglass 1973, 350).

Individuals may have some control over the identity and traits that appear to them as relevant in social encounters although there are considerable variations depending on the traits involved. Dress and images as external signs are perhaps the markers of ethnic and religious affiliation that individuals have the most choice of exhibiting or not. In contrast, there is no possibility of concealing one's background if it is revealed by visible traits such as the colour of the skin. Language may place constraints on the possibility of revealing or concealing one's identity if one has an accent that automatically reveals one's background or, at least, that one's background is different.

Depending on the resources or interests involved in a particular situation– social, political, material, cultural, or "ideal" – different matters may have to be dealt with within the group or in relations with other groups (Deshen 1974). All types can have a religious and/or an ethnic dimension. For instance, political issues can mobilize the religious community when, for example, a political decision concerns a site on which to build a temple or perform a religious ceremony. In such situations – which are frequently controversial – the prominence of the religious identity is enhanced.

Individuals engage in "impression management"[4] in their various social encounters, including those where their ethnic or religious background may have some significance. "What is important is that in a pluralistic society the membership of any ethnic group is aware that outsiders hold stereotypes of them and have knowledge of their content" (Lyman and Douglass 1973, 347). Stereotypes can be positive as well as negative. They may be part of the traditional baggage of images that people have about themselves and of other groups acquired from historical or contemporary inter-group experiences or from international events and relations. "In orienting themselves to the social world of stereotypy in which they live, members of an ethnic group usually attempt some form of collective impression management as they seek to defuse potentially dangerous aspects of the stereotypic saliencies, arouse sympathy for their position as a minority, and influence outsiders toward appreciative and tolerant attitude"(Lyman and Douglass 1973, 347).

The social relevance of an identity and of its cultural dimensions depends in part on the opportunities and constraints for "impression management" and on the skills of individuals in this regard; but it also depends on the societal context and on the circumstances that brought about the encounter. In other words, the salience of ethnicity or religion in the self-conception of individuals and in their social relations tends to be circumstantial. The activation of a particular identity and of specific cultural elements depends on the specific interests and goals involved, that is, on the political, economic, or cultural issues involved.

The relevance of the social context for the management of social-identity management is shown in a comparative study of the experience of Lebanese Muslim immigrants in the United States and Somali Muslim immigrants in Canada (Ajrouch and Kusow 2007). The identity of the two groups of immigrants was based on religious characteristics in their homelands. However, for the Lebanese, religious affiliation placed them in a minority social status position whereas it meant being part of the majority for the Somalis. But their position in the social hierarchy shifted after immigration. The Lebanese became part of the dominant white status group, and the Somalis acquired a visible-minority status.

Whiteness was the preferred social identity for the Lebanese Shi'a Muslims. To be white meant membership in the dominant status group. It also meant being able to assert their status on the basis of their individual qualities as opposed to their membership in a religious group (Ajrouch and Kusow 2007, 82, 84). However, this status position was threatened when they declared their Muslim religious identity, by wearing the *hijab*, for example. Such behaviour put in question their membership in the majority group (85). Thus, their options for managing their social identity were somewhat limited.

The situation of the Somali Muslim immigrants in Canada is quite different. Whereas they were part of the majority status group in their homeland, they become part of a low social-status group in Canada. In addition, a visible-minority status in Canada supersedes any specific cultural and ethnic subcultures that may have existed in the homeland. It is also superimposed on national-origin differences (Sorenson 1991). In contrast, among whites, differences in ethnic and national origin are recognized. However, in relationships of tension with non-white groups, their "whiteness" may render their ethno-cultural differences insignificant.

A study of Iranian immigrants in the United States after the ascent of the Khomeini revolutionary government in Iran also shows that in a negative social and political context, individuals attempt to conceal identities that may place them at a disadvantage. The author argues that "the hostage crisis, coupled with the disenchantment of most Iranians with the revolutionary policies of the Islamic Republic of Iran, caused the identity crisis, identity transformation, and loss or veiling of religious identity among Iranians." In addition, "the anti-Iranian attitudes of most Americans and the anti-Iranian media propaganda that began during the hostage crisis, coupled with American ignorance and refusal to distinguish between pro- and anti-Khomeini Iranians in the US, have also motivated Iranian immigrants to cover up their Iranian national origin" (Mobasher 2006, 101).

The violent events of September 11 had a serious affect on the attitudes and behaviour of Muslims in the United States. Initially, many Muslims attempted to conceal their identity. Women who had been wearing the *hijab*, for example, removed it in order to avoid being objects of hostility. But the opposite can take place. Indeed, Haddad (2007, 253–4) argues that a process of "re-Islamization" has taken place in the aftermath of September 11. This manifested itself in the increasing number of adolescents and young women (daughters of immigrant Muslims) who began wearing the *hijab* and, thus, assuming a public Islamic identity. Faced with the growing negative views of Muslims in the American public, "young American-born Muslim women appear to have appropriated a century old view of the *hijab* as a symbol of solidarity and resistance to efforts to eradicate the religion of Islam ... The re-appropriation of the *hijab* in North America can be seen as a return to authenticity."[5]

Retreating into the Ethno-religious Community

Whatever its source, the feeling of estrangement and of being an outsider is distressing, whether the place where one expects to belong is the workplace, the neighbourhood, the church, the town, or the country. To the extent that immigrants are made to feel like strangers or outsiders, they are likely to "search for a pseudo-extended family through church communities" (Kim 1981, 199).[6] Of course, some may seek a refuge in their ethnic community groups and associations rather than in its religious organizations.

As noted earlier, Kalilombe (1997) found that a Black Christianity developed in a British community in response to the experience of not being welcome in the local church. Hurh and Kim (1990, 31) also observed that the ethnic and religious attachments of Korean Americans as an ethnic and racial minority are partly voluntary but also partly involuntary because of segregation or social exclusion. Such attachments partly explain why Korean Americans are so widely and intensively involved in their ethnic churches.

Religion and commitment to religiously inspired principles may help people deal not only with the expected problems of being transplanted into a new social and cultural milieu but also with exclusion and hostility. It can do so by offering to church members a kind of "social refuge"; a form of defensive community against their perceived marginal status within the larger society (Chong 1998, 262). On the basis of a study of young Muslims in France, Khosrokhavar (1997, 147, 151) suggests that religious involvement can provide a locus of social integration that can counter the negative effects of stigmatization and socio-economic exclusion. As a result, it can also prevent the political radicalization of their anger.

"Downward Assimilation": Living at the Margins of Society

"Downward assimilation" is a type of social marginality (Cao 2005). It results not so much from social rejection and hostility – although these may well be involved – as from a failure of integration. This seems to take place mostly among lower-class male youth. They experience the stresses of transplantation into a new social and economic environment, but kinship ties and community institutions, both secular and religious, fail to integrate them socially, to help them organize their lives, and to assist them with the difficulties of adaptation. As a result, they experience life at the margins.

This situation leads individuals to quit school, spend time in video arcades, and join gangs that provide them with "an identity, a sense of belonging and power as well as further distancing themselves from school, their families, and the mainstream culture." They may be further marginalized by getting into trouble with the law. Since their parents cannot afford to give them money, they join their gang in collecting protection money and, as a result, may be arrested (Cao 2005, 188). They get caught in the spiral of downward assimilation to urban gang culture. This is in contrast with the experience of middle-class youth.

A failure of integration may result from a lack of effective links between the community and the municipal, regional, and federal agencies of the larger society. This factor is suggested by Suttles' (1972) and Kapsis' (1978) analyses of the variations in the degree of anomie in different Black neighbourhoods in the United States. The hypothesis is that communities may be neglected by public agencies because there is no fear of retaliation from a local constituency. In such neglected neighbourhoods, what comes to prevail among segments of their residents are a sense of despair about the future, a perception of normlessness, and low social trust. It seems that this hypothesis is applicable, *mutatis mutandis*, to certain sub-groups who experience the stresses of transplantation into a new social and economic environment. Similar social-psychological processes could take place among categories of individuals (such as lower-class males) who feel that agencies of the larger society are indifferent to their condition.

The Possible Emergence of a Religiously Based Culture of Opposition

Marginalization can involve an experience of alienation or acculturative stress (Berry 1990). In their recent studies comparing adaptation strategies of youth in different countries, Berry and his colleagues (2006) identify prevalent attachment types they term ethnic, national, integrated, and diffuse. The "diffuse" type (with ambiguous attachments) is the least socially integrated. This was observed in the results of the Ethnic Diversity Survey in which respondents who were found to be "marginal" showed the lowest scores on a number of measures of social integration: trust in people generally and in their neighbours, participation in civic organizations or associations, voting in elections, and life satisfaction (Phan and Breton 2010). Social distrust, withdrawal, and even opposition to the society may be manifestations of a lack of social integration.

An important reason for the development of distrust and opposition among some members of religious minorities is "that religious groups function according to the same principles as political, ethnic and other groups" (Jackson and Hunsberger 1999, 510).[7] Thus, when religious groups vie for collective self-esteem, political representation, or economic opportunities or for the promotion of their values and customs (in the school curriculum or in church services, for example), their initiatives can generate negative attitudes towards other groups. This, of course, may occur among some members of both majority and minority religious groups (Jackson and Hunsberger 1999, 510, 519).[8]

Members of a group who affirm their identity and culture in a confrontation with another group or with an institution are not necessarily driven by religion. Rather, more often than not, they are reacting to a lack of access to social, economic, or political resources – in short, to a lack of social integration. In-depth profiles of terrorists and radicals have revealed that all have experienced some social exclusion and that many feel some disconnection from their local community and have lived through an identity crisis (Bartlett et al. 2010, 8–10).

Religion may act as a mobilizing element if the alienated group is a religious minority. In such instances, religion provides those who are challenging the existing distribution of resources and institutional arrangements and practices with a motivational resource, that is, the sense of pursuing a worthwhile cause. Exclusion and discrimination may generate a rejection of the larger society and foster a religiously based culture of opposition. The religious culture may provide a paradigm of *resistance*[9] in certain segments of the religious minority. Often, however, the goals of the social mobilization and protest are not specifically religious but rather social, economic, and political. Mobilization and protest tend to involve pronounced distrust of governments and intense negative feelings toward their foreign policies (Bartlett et al. 2010).[10]

Religion can also have the opposite effect, as when it acts in such a way as to prevent individuals from engaging in socially destructive behaviour. Among the young in France, there is an Islam that is seen as condemning violence. Islamic organizations and social networks are a substitute for other forms of organization, such as political parties and labour unions. The religious takes over and "gives meaning to the young who are by and large in situations of insecurity and even of social exclusion" (Khosrokhavar 1997, 25, my translation). Bartlett and his colleagues (2010, 12) also point out that their study revealed that Muslim communities were undertaking self-policing within their own communities to identify and dissuade individuals contemplating violent acts.

No doubt, there is much variation in this regard. Not all religions develop communal forms that can help the poorly integrated in the ethnic community to cope with the barriers they encounter in their attempts to become integrated in the society and institutions.

CONCLUSION

Newcomers may encounter resistance and even opposition as they attempt to establish roots in the society of adoption. Some members of the receiving society may perceive the newcomers as a threat to their collective identity, way of life, social cohesion, and organizational practices. And the greater the perceived cultural difference between the incoming groups and the receiving society, the more pronounced the resistance.

There may be different reactions to what is experienced as social distance and even exclusion. Members of the minority may become more aware of their religion since it serves as a basis of social differentiation; a marker of "we" and "they." Their religious beliefs and practices may acquire a new significance for them. This may, in turn, accentuate their social marginality and bring about a retreat into the ethno-religious community. It can also lead some members of the minority to distance themselves from their community in order to avoid derogatory experiences.

Exclusion and discrimination may generate a rejection of the larger society and foster a religiously based culture of opposition or a paradigm of *resistance*[11] in certain segments of the religious minority – a situation that contains the potential for conflict.

Finally, marginality may be the outcome of a failure of integration, a phenomenon that seems to occur primarily among lower-class male youth. The lack of social support from either a religious or secular community may make it quite difficult for individuals to organize their lives and to cope with the difficulties of adaptation. As a result, they experience life at the margins.

PART TWO

Transformations Resulting from Embeddedness in the New Cultural Environment

Religion and religious organizations can play an important role with regard to the problems and challenges of social and cultural transplantation – a role that may last for a more or less long time. However, as immigrants and especially their descendants attempt to become full participants in the new social and institutional environment, the ways in which they regard and experience their religion may also change. As they become more and more embedded in the mainstream society and are increasingly subjected to its social and cultural influences, new issues emerge with regard to the interconnection between elements of their religious and of their ethnic cultures. In addition, their personal beliefs and practices may change, and their relationship with their ethno-religious community may evolve.

3

The Dissociation of Religion and Ethnicity

Analytically, religion and ethnicity are two distinct phenomena. "Religion involves some conception of a supernatural being, world, or force, and a notion that the supernatural is active, that events and conditions here on earth are influenced by the supernatural (Stark and Bainbridge 1985, 5). Religions differ in the doctrines that spell out these conceptions of the supernatural and its relation to worldly events and conditions. Religious groups are formed on the basis of particular doctrines.

A commitment to a particular religion and religious group can have several dimensions: belief or the acceptance of the doctrine; practice, which includes acts of worship and devotion toward the supernatural; experience of a sense of particular awareness or contact with the supernatural (for example, a "born-again" experience); knowledge of central elements of the religious culture; and consequences, that is, actions in everyday life (such as prescribed and prohibited behaviour) (Stark and Bainbridge 1985, 9–10).

Definitions of ethnicity can include "objective" and "subjective" elements. The first refers to a real or presumed common origin or descent, historical experiences, and cultural heritage, which may include religion. A distinctive ethnicity can be expressed in customs, language, values and norms, and a set of symbols. These may include both secular and religious components – religious in the sense described above and secular in the sense of that they have no connection with the supernatural in the culture of the group and of its members.

The "subjective" dimension refers to the fact that "objective" descent and historical and cultural factors are important in community formation only in so far as individuals attach significance to them in differentiating themselves from others and in shaping their in-group and out-group relationships and orienting their day-to-day behaviour. At the collective level, the term "subjective" may not be entirely accurate; the expression "socially significant" may be closer to what Barth (1969, 14) means when he argues that the features that matter are "those which the actors themselves regard as significant ... as signals and emblems of differences" from other groups, that is, to mark their social boundaries. These features may include religious beliefs, values and norms, and ritual practices.

The process through which particular cultural features become socially significant can be seen as an adaptation to particular circumstances that members of the group must make at some point and in a particular social context. This is likely to be the case for ethnic and religious minorities who become immigrants. Thus, there may not be a simple process of dissociation between secular and religious cultural features but a new combination of different ethnic and religious elements. In other words, the subjective or socially significant dimension is the most useful for dealing with the relationship between religious and ethnic identity. What do people – members of religious minorities as well as of the mainstream society – consider to be their religious heritage? Is the sense of their origin, history, cultural values, world views, and customs so intertwined in their minds and lives with religious beliefs and practices that they constitute a single cultural package (Chong 1998, 264; Eid 2003)? In other words, it is possible for the religious factor to be a more or less important cultural element in the formation and maintenance of an ethnic group (Szajkowski 1997, 29).

But it is important to emphasize, as does Barot (1993, 7) that "sociologists and anthropologists who identify ethnicity as a phenomenon of prime importance may argue that the religion members of a group pursue is integral to their ethnicity ... Although it is perfectly possible to show that links do exist between a particular group and their religion in specific cases, there is no more a one-to-one relationship between ethnicity and religion than there ever was between race and culture."

This approach can also be applied to religious groups: ethnic elements can be more or less significant in the creation and maintenance of a religious identity and community. And the relationship can be reciprocal in that religious elements can define and support a distinct ethno-cultural identity while the socially significant elements of the ethnocultural background may define and support a particular religious identity and commitment.

As Goldscheider (2009a, 2009b) suggests, such an integration of both kinds of elements may be particularly significant among Jews. Because of their ethnic identity and culture, Jews are not simply a religious group like Catholics and Muslims. Judaism readily incorporates the secular. But because of their religious culture, Jewish Americans are not an ethnic group like Italian and Hispanic Americans. Thus, the fundamental dichotomy between religious and ethnic identity is not as useful among Jews as it is among other groups (2009a, 268). Variations across various religious collectivities in different social and historical contexts need to be examined empirically.

But it is also possible that, with time and changing circumstances, religion and ethnic culture can become largely dissociated from each other and that individuals will recognize that their ethnic culture and customs are distinct from their religious doctrine, moral principles, and practices. This does not mean that either set of cultural elements is abandoned; some of both may retain some importance for a minority. The hypothesis is that, with time, members come to see them as two distinct bases for their individual identities and for the identity of their community. In addition, individuals may come to realize that they could change religious affiliation without changing their ethnic identity and attachments or that they can become highly acculturated without abandoning their religious affiliation, as frequently happens. The blending and the dissociation of ethnicity and religion as bases of social identities and affiliations are the subject of this chapter.[1]

It is important to distinguish between two manifestations of the relationship between religion and ethnicity. One pertains to the correlation between ethnic identity and religious affiliation of individuals. That question is considered in the next chapter.

The dimension of the relation between religion and ethnicity considered here is whether elements of the ethnically based conceptions of the world and society are infused with religious meaning, whether the personal, family, and social norms are defined as moral obligations by a religious doctrine and a system of moral principles; and whether elements of the religious rituals and practices have been "borrowed" from the ethnic culture. In other words, are the two cultures – secular and religious – intimately intertwined or are they distinct in people's minds and day-to-day decisions in the conduct of their lives?

It should be emphasized that the hypothesis is not that the elements of the culture of a community are classified objectively into religious and secular categories, either by individuals or by the community. Rather, the process of dissociation and its outcome are subjective phenomena at the level of individuals, and social and perhaps even political at the level of the community. To the extent that individuals make a distinction or communities reach a consensus, it may or may not be once and for all. It may change as circumstances change and new issues need to be addressed.

THE BLENDING OR INTERWEAVING OF ETHNIC AND RELIGIOUS CULTURES

The blending of religion and ethnicity implies that the two cannot be empirically dissociated from one another but are experienced as an undifferentiated whole (Ajrouch 1999; McLellan 2004; Amarasingam 2008). To the extent that this is the case, both religious and ethnic practices and institutions play mutually reinforcing roles in shaping the identity of individuals and in the formation and vitality of ethno-religious communities. The culture and language of the group can also be seen as essential for the maintenance of the religious commitment and practice among members. In traditional French-Canadian society, for example, a standard motto was "La langue est la gardienne de la foi" (language is the guardian of the faith).

Religious ceremonies can – besides their religious dimension – be a vehicle for the transmission of a particular culture and language and for the sharing of a common identity (Boisvert 2005, 77). "When we consider what Canadian Sikh leaders and spokesmen say and do – in *gurdwaras*, associations, etc. – what we find is a very strong emphasis on ethnic identity, even when appealing to explicitly religious beliefs, symbols, and rites to support that identity" (O'Connell 2000, 194–5). Hence the finding that those who identify with their ethnic churches tend to have a higher rate of mother-tongue retention than those who convert to mainstream Canadian Protestant churches (Wang 2002).

There are, of course, variations among religious collectivities in the extent to which ethnic elements are considered by adherents to be part of their religion and religious elements to be part of their ethnoculture. A relevant factor may be the extent to which a religion is or was historically embedded in the culture of the country or region of origin (Ajrouch 1999, 136), as in the case of Christianity in Western Europe and North America, Hinduism in India, Islam in some Middle Eastern countries, and so on. It has been observed that for Christians, Muslims, and Jews from the Middle East, the religious affiliation determines the individual and collective identity. A person is born, grows up, and dies in a specific religious community. For instance, the *millet* system devised by the Ottomans to govern their domain structured the social and political order along religious lines. Muslim and non-Muslim groups were given some autonomy in the organization of the lives of their adherents" (Haddad, 1994, 65). Faith and ethnic and political affiliations were intermingled in the organization and unfolding of individual and community lives.

There are also groups, such as Indian Hindu immigrants, who practise "domestic religion" in which several religious rituals are practised at home. In his study of Indian Hindu and Korean

Protestant immigrants, Min found that religious values and rituals are inseparably tied to ethnic customs, including funerals, weddings, holidays, food, music, and dance. What predominates involves more family and small-group rituals than participation in a congregation. The interweaving of ethnic and religious culture is maintained almost daily (Min 2005, 100). That is also the case among the Chinese, whose religion is indistinguishable from a number of distinctive characteristics of Chinese culture. Chinese religion is focused on the family; it has less public presence. Family religion is basic; individual and communal religion are secondary (Lai et al. 2005, 91–4).

Among the Hindus, the observing of religious holidays and performing of ceremonies on auspicious family occasions with *puja*, traditional food, and flowers is essential. It is more important than reading and interpreting sacred texts. In contrast, Protestantism puts far more emphasis on reading the Bible and listening to the pastor's sermons than on performing informal rituals at home. As a result, there is a stronger association between religion and ethnic or national culture among the Indian Hindu community than among Korean Protestants (Min 2005, 117).

Another variation in the connection between religious and ethnic cultures concerns the norms defining the place and role of men and women in the family, community, and society. These norms and institutionalized patterns may be cultural as well as sanctioned or perceived to be sanctioned by the religion. Religion, which is seen as having a supernatural validity, is used to safeguard the culture. Thus the cultural heritage as regards gender is perceived and experienced as ethno-religious. In particular it is the role of women that tends to be central in these traditional patterns and in the definition of the collective identity. In certain Muslim countries, for example, nation, religion, and gender are intertwined in the definition of the collective identity (Eid 2007, 57ff). The role of women is a critical element in establishing the cultural and religious distinctiveness of the group. Women are seen as the main bearers of the ethno-religious identity and traditions. This attitude may persist once they have migrated to Western countries. Women are assigned a central role in the maintenance of the ethno-religious culture of the community. As a result, they face intense anti-assimilation pressures from their families and community (Ajrouch 1999, 138).

But the degree to which ethnicity and religion are interwoven may be different in the religious traditions that include little ethnic diversity (for example, Sikhism and Chinese religion) than in those that are ethnically heterogeneous (for example, Islam and Christianity). In culturally homogeneous traditions, the blending could be expected to be relatively high in contrast with the traditions whose adherents are from different ethnic origins. Because different elements of the religious doctrine or practices are selected or emphasized so as to "fit" the cultural particularity of each ethnic group, adherents may be more likely to see a difference between the religious and secular components. But this is not necessarily the case. The Irish, African, French, or Chinese who practise their Christianity differently, for example, may not be aware of these differences or may feel that their way is the most authentic. But this is definitely an empirical question.

There can be considerable variation not only between but also within religious collectivities. Through an analysis of the literature – academic writing, creative literature, and written defences (apologias), Loewen (2008) identifies six distinctive approaches to the question of how ethnicity and religion are intertwined for Mennonites.

In the first, precedence is given to ethnicity. Religious tradition is de-emphasized, critiqued, or sometimes rejected. A second group of writers, mostly urbanized Mennonites, celebrate a Mennonite ethnicity but show "a disinterest and even disdain for traditional Mennonite religiousness"; rather they link themselves to Canadian evangelicalism (Loewen, 2008: 349). A third category might be called "neo-Anabaptists." They are urban thinkers who also separate ethnicity from religious faith: they call their faith Mennonite or Anabaptist, but "they are guarded on Mennonite ethnicity" (351). A Mennonite faith and a Mennonite ethnicity are directly linked in a fourth group of writers. A fifth group, which may represent the quiet majority, consists of those for whom "Mennonite ethnicity is 'symbolic' and without religious significance, but seems to exist almost naturally alongside Mennonite religious faith" (354). The sixth group of writers focus on newly arrived immigrants who call themselves Mennonites but for whom Mennonite ethnicity or Anabaptist religious ideals are not meaningful. Scholars argue that these individuals identify as Mennonites "for reasons of friendship, gratitude, and even a strategy of integrating into a highly respected social sector of middle-class Canada" (356).

Besides the background brought from the culture of origin, the experience in the adopted country may also be important in the blending of ethnicity and religion. In her analysis of a Korean community, Chong (1998) notes that, as opposed to the "transplanted" ethnicity of the first generation, ethnicity for the second generation is primarily an emergent phenomenon that incorporates, appropriates, and in part reshapes the cultural attributes of the first generation in ways that are more than simply abstract or symbolic. This is accomplished in the ethnic church by ideologically legitimizing and defending a set of core traditional Korean values and forms of social relationships that constitute the main components of the second-generation ethnicity. Religion serves to legitimize certain orientations, beliefs, and practices. It offers interpretations of reality, rules, and legitimations that define identity. Chong (1998, 265) refers to this process as "sacralization."

The blending of religion and ethnic culture can also have practical consequences. Chen (2006, 574) points out that the main reason for involvement by the Chinese in the evangelical church (after moving to the US) was to make sure their children were "on the right track." It was to solve the intergenerational tensions that arise in immigrant families. More generally, it was to protect the children from lax sexual standards, a consumer-oriented culture, and the associated patterns of behaviour found in the surrounding society. This also included school violence, drug abuse, and teenage pregnancies.

To people from Confucian traditions, filial piety is a central moral principle that should guide human behaviour. However, parents know that it is not possible to re-create the Confucian culture and life patterns in North America. They realize that the qualities needed to succeed in the United States are "independence, aggressiveness, and courage while in Taiwan it is studiousness, hard work and obedience" (Chen 2006, 582). The tension between Chinese traditions of collectivism and American individualism are constant family-related themes in the Chinese church. These parents are in a dilemma. Confucian principles have lost their moral legitimacy within the family; yet there is the view that mainstream America, which is considered to be morally bankrupt, does not offer more attractive models for the family. Religion helps to resolve the dilemma. First, the church is seen as a moral bastion in an otherwise immoral society. Second, it helps to maintain parental authority. "Rather than the Confucian language of indebtedness and obligation, immigrant parents use the moral language of Christian discipleship to achieve traditionally Confucian ends." There is a shift from family duty to Christian discipleship. The source of authority is not in the parents themselves, but the Bible. Thus, religion serves to blend Confucian traditions and patterns of social relationships with the cultural imperatives of the social environment (Chen 2006, 584, 587–8).

Within a religion, there are usually variations among individuals and sub-groups. Since some choice is involved, at least in a pluralistic context such as exist in Western societies, individuals differ from each other even if the religious affiliation is experienced as an ascribed element of one's personality. However, as Cadge and Davidman (2006, 24–5) point out, rather than seeing their religious identities as either ascribed by birth or achieved through conscious choices, respondents[2] often fall along a continuum between these two conceptual categories. For instance, most of the first-generation Buddhists interviewed for the study combine ideas about being Buddhist based on their birth with ideas based on Buddhist practices.

But the Buddhists whose sole identification was ascriptive saw their religion as inseparable from their nationality. In contrast, the Jewish respondents whose sole identification was ascriptive did not see Judaism as a religion or a nationality but rather as a cultural, ethnic, and historical identity. For them, their Jewishness is a matter of birth and does not necessarily involve practising any of the rituals of Judaism or adhering to any of its religious tenets (2006, 32).

This finding suggests that the formation of a defensive community as a response to the experience of social exclusion can have the effect of blending ethnicity and religion. Religion and church membership offer community members "a form of defensive ethnicity against their perceived 'marginal' status within American society as a non-white minority group ... a kind of 'refuge' from this sense of marginalization, and along with it, positive social identity and group empowerment" (Chong 1998, 262).

Inter-ethnic or interracial tensions or conflicts can also lead to a reinforcement of the association of a particular expression of the religion with the identity and culture of a group. Kalilombe (1997, 307, 310–12), for instance, found that "black Christianity developed in response to the need for black Christians to make sense of the state of "ethnic minority" imposed on them when they came to Britain" (307). Their expectations as newcomers were not met; they discovered that they were not welcome. This feeling was reinforced by the differences in church style. They found the white congregation quite "cold"; that its members were fulfilling some sort of duty; that they seemed to see that life was really about other things such as material well-being, good jobs, money, success, or enjoyment (322). The response was to form Black congregations in which the religious expression would be given more prominence and that would help them to cope with exclusion and hostility.

In such situations, religion becomes "ethnicized" in the sense that group bonding is based on both religious and secular values and that both community members and outsiders see them as intrinsically intertwined. The "ethnicization" of religion in such circumstances could be taken as an indication of a lack of social integration into mainstream society. This also appears to be the case with a number of Muslim communities in Europe and North America. The ethnicization of religion may be more likely when the identity is imposed from the outside as when, for example, (as noted in the previous chapter) individuals from Middle Eastern countries are categorized according to their religious affiliation rather than their national or ethnic origin. The religion may not matter very much for them, but they are forced into that communal identity (which may have been one they sought to abandon when leaving their country of origin). According to Nielsen (1991, 53) "the pressure imposed on Muslim organizations by European official legal, political and bureaucratic expectations, is such that Islam has to become an ethnic identity. This may not be serious for some religious groups (such as Sikhs) but it is serious for Muslims who come from different ethnic backgrounds. It is also serious in inadvertently imposing an ethnic restriction on a religion which by it nature is a universal religion."

Events on the international scene can play a significant role in this connection. Khosrokhavar (1997) observed that the young people's "inclination for Islamist activism or proselytism is not necessarily tied to a regular religious practice but is influenced by circumstances in which extra-religious events – the 1991 Gulf War, the veil affair of 1989 and 1994 ... and the growing feeling of injustice and racism towards young immigrants – emphasize the sense of belonging to an identity that is not Arab, Turkish, or North African (Maghrébine), but Islamist, even radical Islamist" (30, my translation). Thus the Islam of exclusion that can be seen as a form of protest against existing social barriers is frequently a non-religious Islam (212).

In such cases, religion becomes "secularized" in the sense that the social differentiation takes place along religious lines but the religious content does not have much relevance for the individuals involved.[3] The religious factor may act as a sort of code, a set of rigid rites and precepts that individuals simply endorse without giving them any dynamic meaning. "Such a phenomenon should perhaps not be taken as an indicator of a revival of religious interest on the part of the young but rather as an indication of the ethnicization of the religious factor, since it tends more and more to have no other function than to assure the survival of the community with which ties should definitely be maintained when in a precarious social situation" (Bastenier 1998, 212, my translation).

Negative representations of minority religions and the perception of their values and practices as incompatible with "Canadian values" can make it harder for their members to dissociate their religious from their ethnic identity. In his study of Moroccan immigrants in Belgium, Bastenier (1998, 204–6) notes that their belonging to an Arabic-Islamic community accounts in their own eyes for the rejection to which they are subjected, a rejection that is partly based on international events in which Islam is cast in a negative role. Their ethno-religious defensive re-identification derives from their experience as immigrants and not from their village or regional background.

Finally, members of the larger society frequently do not distinguish between the ethnic and religious elements of a minority's culture. In such situations, the blending is "imposed" from the outside or supported by external attitudes.

THE DISSOCIATION OF RELIGION AND ETHNICITY

Even if ethnic identity, culture, and customs are in fact often intertwined with religious beliefs and practices in such a way that they constitute a single cultural package, the two are analytically distinct and can be dissociated in people's minds and lives and in the organization of their communities. For instance, a distinction has been made between Islamic and Muslim institutions. *Islamic* institutions are considered as "absolutely vital to people being able to practice Islam as a religion in a correct way ... Examples of institutions in this category include mosques, prayer halls and the essential conditions for the proper performance of slaughter, circumcision, weddings, funerals, etc. ... the necessary conditions for the availability of religious leaders ... In contrast, *Muslim* institutions are those "which (at least traditionally) constitute important parts of life in Muslim societies at the same time as their existence ... *cannot* be said to be *obligatory* or *recommended*" (Sander 1991, 69; emphasis in original).

Gitelman (2009, 307) points out that some elements such as dietary laws and prohibitions on the consumption of alcohol, clothing (nothing prescribed or proscribed), and economic behaviour are relatively easily dissociated from the religious beliefs and values. This is in contrast to attitudes and norms pertaining, for example, to gender roles and relations and sexual behaviour. Some members of a religious group may think these are not inherent to their religion while others may think that being a good Christian, Muslim, Hindu, and so on necessarily implies adhering to religiously prescribed beliefs and norms. In short, the "sacred" and the "secular" always tend to have an impact on each other. In modern societies, the separation of the two is considerable, but it is not complete.

The Impact of the Political and Cultural Context

While the blending of religious and ethnocultural elements is more easily maintained under conditions of social and geographic isolation, the process of dissociation tends to be triggered by increased interaction with the larger society. This is especially the case if certain features of the minority culture are perceived as undesirable or incompatible with those of the majority culture and if the larger society is religiously and culturally pluralistic. In such circumstances, members of the minority religious community are often confronted with cultural ambiguities and dilemmas.

First, as noted above, negative judgments of a group's beliefs and practices by members of the larger society may trigger a defensive response. Defending one's religion from what is perceived and experienced as a negative characterization, especially in the media, may become an important part of the contemporary identity politics of the religious minority (Jacobsen 2005, 159). The defence may consist of claims that the supposedly objectionable elements are not intrinsic parts of the religion; that they are not included in the founding sources of the religion but rather are specific to a particular national or ethnic culture. Of course, there may be considerable debate within the religious group as to what the true beliefs and the essential practices of the religion are – a debate that may never be definitely resolved in the sense that a consensus may never be reached, at least not on all the beliefs and norms in contention. However, the debate itself shows that attempts are made to dissociate the elements that are religious from those that are not.

Second, the experience of cultural diversity is relevant in this connection. The differences between the culture of the adopted society and that of the region or country of origin tend to lead immigrants to distinguish between the elements of their religious and of their ethnocultural or national traditions, between what defines them as belonging to a particular religion in contrast to a particular ethnic culture (such as being Catholic and Irish, Muslim and Iranian, or Buddhist and Kmer (Bramadat and Seljak 2005, 18; Boisvert, 2005, 80). Frequent encounters between people of different religious and cultural backgrounds would tend to lead people to such an examination of their beliefs and practices. As could be expected, such sensitivity would tend to be stronger among members of the second generation and to increase with the level of education.

In general, major religions are framed in such a way as to have a universal relevance and applicability. In contrast, ethnic cultural elements have relevance primarily, if not exclusively, in the life of a particular people. Religious ideals are not meant to be confined to any particular country or group but to apply to the world. This can be a powerful motivating force for individuals. Jacobson (1997, 244) observed that their religious affiliation allowed young Muslims to feel that they are part of a "worldwide trend which links them politically and financially to the global *umma*." This sense of a widely encompassing community underscores the peculiarities of their ethnic or national background in contrast to the defining elements of their "universal" religion.

In addition, the social boundaries that encompass expressions of religious identity are pervasive and clear-cut. In Islam, "the emphasis on rightful action means that to be a devout Muslim one must behave in certain, explicitly defined ways; and therefore a Muslim is obliged to express his belonging to the Muslim

community ... Thus, the social differences that distinguish observant Muslims from non-Muslims tend to be demonstrated in
normal interaction and on an ongoing basis, rather than merely
from time to time. In contrast, the boundaries defining ethnic
identity are semi-permeable. Accordingly, they are increasingly
easier to cross in most social situations, except in instances where
racist ideas about differences prevail" (Jacobson, 1997, 248).

The Role of Inter-generational Interaction

The process of "negotiation" between members of the immigrant
and of second generations can make individuals sensitive to what
is religious and what is cultural. Children socialized into somewhat different religious and ethnic values and traditions from
those of their parents frequently "bargain" with their parents as
to the behaviour that is acceptable from the point of view of
both sets of cultural expectations. In the process, what is ethnic
and what is religious may become apparent to both (Kucukcan
1998, 128). Clarke (1998, 150) found that some Muslims use the
Qur'an to question assumptions about what is and what is not
Islamic and to question the cultural practices passed on to them
by their parents as associated with Islam. Such questioning is
carried out for the purpose of constructing an Islam more in
keeping with their needs and identity as Muslims born and educated as Europeans.

Initially many immigrants may find themselves confused as
to whether particular behavioural codes or prescriptions derive from cultural customs or religious, as Barazangi (1989,
75) observed among Arab Muslim immigrants. Such confusion is part of the "cognitive dissonance" that frequently
characterizes the experience of immigrants who feel the need
to reconcile the sometimes dissonant attitudes and behaviour
demanded by the three environments in which they practise
them: the home, the Muslim-Arab community, and the host
society. In addition, the dissonance is somewhat different for
parents and children. Parents need to adjust an existing belief
system and a particular attachment to the "Arabic" heritage

to their living experience in the secular West, while their children need to integrate the belief system transmitted by their parents, the Arabic sentiment derived by their community membership, and the secular system of the society at large (67, 69).

Women at the Centre of Cross-pressures

One of the main changes involved in the process of acculturation is the redefinition of gender roles and relationships. In this process, women may be more prone than men to distinguish between what is religiously prescribed and what are elements stemming from their particular ethno-culture. As noted above, the cultural conceptions of gender roles and the related prescriptions are frequently sanctioned by religion. But these prescriptions tend to place many more obligations and restrictions on women than on men and to assign women a lower status. Also, women are assigned a more crucial role than men in maintaining the "authentic" ethnic identity and its continuity of the family and community. They are also central to the social and moral order of the society to such an extent that moral deviance on their part is seen as a threat to the good functioning not only of the family but also of the community (Timmerman 2000, 18, 22).

Timmerman (2000, 22) points out that in Muslim countries Islam offers the only legitimate framework for debating the social position of women. The gender equality professed (but frequently not fully practised) in Western societies provides another socially sanctioned framework. Such an alternative constitutes an invitation to women from inegalitarian traditions to redefine their roles to fit the new socio-cultural context. Such a process would require a removal of the religious and cultural justifications of the inequality and a reformulation of religious principles and prescriptions derived from a new reading of the original sources.

Again, this would be especially so among the well educated. Women with higher levels of education are more likely to make a distinction between Qu'ranic teaching and that which has cultural roots (Macey 1999, 859). This is perhaps because it is the gender roles that are most strikingly different between non-Western and Western cultures. Consistent with these observations are findings in a study of Arab women in the United States that among those with inegalitarian gender attitudes, their affiliations as Muslims and Christians are less important in shaping these attitudes than the degree of their religiosity and of their ethnic attachment (Read 2003).

In an acculturation study of Moroccan immigrants in the Netherlands, the moderate attachment to both Moroccan and Dutch cultures that was observed among female respondents might be seen as an ambivalent acculturation pattern. On the one hand, women respondents increasingly oppose the gender inequality in their culture. This is especially so among member of the younger generation who are engaged in the process of eman-cipation. Yet most of them do not want to risk their family and community bonds and turn their backs on the heritage of their culture altogether (Stevens et al. 2004, 699). This seems to imply that a distinction is made between the religious requirement and the cultural prescription.

In some cases, the association of customs with religion can lead some women to develop negative feeling towards their reli-gion. One of Nayar's female respondents said, "Because I associ-ated the customs with religion, I had a negative feeling towards Sikhism – not allowed to go out, wearing Punjabi suit in the home, cooking and cleaning in the home for my brothers" (Nayar 2004, 143).

Religious symbols can sometimes serve more general social purposes, as in the case of women who have made the conscious decision to wear the *hijab* but do not see themselves as oppressed or marginalized. "On the contrary, many become activists while keeping the outer signs of conformity to religious traditions and by following principles and methods that are widely accepted as Islamic. This is certainly true in the Norwegian context where the hijab confers upon those who wear it liberty of movement and a certain independence and authority in relation to families and communities" (Naguib 2002, 170; see also Timmerman

2000, 24). In other words, what is seen as a symbol of oppression is used to facilitate the process of social liberation.

The display of religious symbols can thus have different meanings in public-sphere behaviour. The *hijab* as a symbol of solidarity in the face of hostility was mentioned earlier (Haddad 2007). Also, "the wearing of the head scarf by Muslim women, for example, can be a protest against the norms and values of the Western world ... Similarly, discarding the head scarf can be a statement to the Muslim community in which they live of their readiness to live by the Qur'an alone and not by customs and traditions that have no basis therein" (Clarke 1998, 150).

Depending on the situation, then, individuals may or may not find it advantageous to reveal their religious affiliation or its importance to them. In certain religions, such flexibility is available to both men and women; in some it is primarily available to one or the other.

Evolution over Generations

With time and especially generations, it seems that the distinction between what is properly religious and what derives from their particular ethnic culture becomes recognized and accepted. Members of the second generation are perhaps especially likely to experience the cultural contrast in their own families because they were born, or at least educated, in a Western environment but are living with parents who have a non-Western origin.

And, as will be seen later, religion becomes progressively relegated to the private sphere and compartmentalized from day-to-day secular life, a process that tends to be more pronounced among second and subsequent generations. Referring to Muslim youth, Barazangi (1989, 70) notes that "as they are primarily Americanized, their understanding of Islam is influenced by the Western ontological and epistemological worldview, and they tend to practice their perception of Islam within the framework of the American values."

According to Barth (1969, 14), the cultural content of ethnic dichotomies is of two orders. First, there are overt signals or signs, such as dress, language, house form, or general style of life.

Second, there are basic value orientations and standards of morality and excellence by which performance is judged. Chong (1998, 269) argues that for the second generation, the latter are the ones that matter most as markers of ethnicity. The hypothesis is that individuals would make the same distinction in the area of religious behaviour: overt signals or signs would tend to include ethnic elements while basic value orientations would be more closely defined in terms of the basic religious doctrine.

The distinction between the particularism of ethnicity and the universalism of religion is another way of looking at this distinction. On the one hand, major world religions purport to have universal relevance and applicability. They also serve to orient behaviour in all spheres of life and therefore demand of their adherents a self-conscious and explicit commitment. In addition, with the technological possibilities of transnational communication and awareness, the formation and evolution of religious identities in a Western context become inseparable from the circumstances of the transnational existence of the religion.[4] On the other hand, *ethnic culture* is an aspect of life that relates to a particular people and a particular place (Jacobson 1997, 239). *Religion*, on the other hand, would be seen as important because it is about what one thinks, not what country one comes from. The "collective ideal" contained within religious rhetoric is not confined to a particular country but is meant to encompass the world – and this is can be a powerful motivating force. Islam, for example, allows young people in Britain to feel that they are part of a "worldwide trend which links them politically and financially to the global *umma* (244–5). In short, to the extent that religious identities are globalized and redefined within and between states, national and ethnic boundaries will tend to be transcended (McLellan 1999, 212).

It is also possible that the cultural elements ingrained in the religion are considered irrelevant in the new societal context. Vertovec (1990) observed that many youth experience a "crisis of relevance" of the Brahman-dominated religious practices in Britain. This crisis also includes a gap between them and the immigrant generation. This may also have been the case with the young British Pakistanis studied by Jacobson (1997), who see that there is a wide range of behaviour that is traditional or cultural rather than religious. They differentiate between culture and what is "true" Islam, stressing that religion is more important in their lives than their ethnic affiliation.

Another illustration is the case of the Hindu youth movement in Britain to which many members of the Hindu community belonged – a movement that provided a renewed appreciation, not only for religious reasoning and ritual practices, but also for what are consciously identified as Hindu ideals of domestic and other areas of life. Religion does not furnish the criteria for ethnic consciousness solely to promote communal interests in terms of equity in status and resource control. It has also underscored very personal religious sentiments, day-to-day values, and family ideals (Vertovec, 1990, 239, 246, 247).

An interesting example of dissociation of religion and culture is a re-interpretation of Hindu ideas such as, for example, the caste system: the new interpretation distinguishes between birthright and rights derived from individual merit and effort. That is, one's characteristics and inner drive rather than birth determine caste. This is "a contestable view, yet it remains an interesting attempt to merge egalitarianism with the more hierarchical implications of the caste system" (Banerjee and Coward 2005, 44). It was also observed that "some parents draw on new political movements in India to facilitate the acculturation of their children. The rise of Hindu nationalism articulated in India by organizations such as the Bharatiya Janata Party … has provided many Hindu parents in Canada and the US with a conduit for the socialization of their children in a certain interpretation of Hindu identity as well as perpetuating this identity within a multicultural context in North America." In Hindu nationalism, "the Hindu self is seen as tolerant, peace-loving, devoted to gender equality" (45). The parents' purpose is to show that particular interpretations of Hinduism are not inherent in the religion itself; rather they are associated with particular social groups and classes. There are indeed movements in India that challenge the cultural dominance of the monolithic North Indian, upper-caste, upper-class interpretation of Hinduism (Banerjee and Coward 2005).

Nayar (2004, 136) observed that among Sikhs in Vancouver, the first generation treats religion as inseparable from culture; thus it is likely to treat customs such as arranged marriage as part of religion. But this association begins to break down with the second generation. The third generation tends to develop "the analytics mode of thinking," and to the extent that this is the case, "they are able to articulate their frustration that Punjabi customs are being passed down from their parents as religion, when in fact, *these customs are often in direct contradiction* to the spiritual teachings" (143–4; emphasis in original).

Some young Muslims emphasize Islamic rather than ethnic responsibilities in order to separate themselves from their parents' culture. "Since they see Islam as a universal religion, they stress what they see as Islamic values rather than ethnic cultural practices. Furthermore, defining Islam in this way, rather than as tied to one particular ethnicity, young Muslims also have a larger pool from which to choose marriage partners" (McDonough and Hoodfar, 2005, 154).

The notion of "peoplehood" or community is very important to groups such as the Mennonites. For them, traditionally, peoplehood implied both religious and ethnic identities that have been historically fused as a result of their long history of diaspora (Winland 1993, 117). Among Mennonites in Canada, the German language has been seen as essential for the maintenance of an ethno-religious identity (Redekop 1992). But over time, adjustments have been and continue to be made to the secular surroundings. These adjustments require a new articulation of a comprehensive and meaningful notion of peoplehood that entails difficult and sometimes socially divisive choices between two key components of Mennonite identity: religion and ethnicity (Winland 1993, 117–18). However, in at least some cases, "it is perhaps more accurate to speak in terms of a synthesis of faith, culture and community giving way to one another, rather than posing an ethnicity-to-religion 'progression' too starkly" (Redekop 1992, 35). That is, what may emerge are varying combinations of religious and ethno-cultural elements.

The Impact of Religious Conversion

The dissociation of religion from ethnicity is perhaps most apparent in the case of conversion to a mainstream religion (Christianity in North America). As will be seen in chapter 4, there may be several reasons that individuals change their religious affiliation. But whatever the reasons, it is a process that is likely to lead those who undergo the experience to distinguish between their religious beliefs and practices and the elements of their ethnic background.

CONCLUSION

The process of integration into a new socio-cultural environment can lead to new perspectives on one's religion. In particular, individuals may ask if some of their religious beliefs and practices are properly religious or if they derive from their ethnic or national culture. It should be emphasized that the blending or dissociation of religion and ethnicity is a question of degree. It is also a subjective phenomenon. It may be observed by outsiders, but what matters is what happens in the minds and behaviour of members of the religious community. It is also subjective in the sense that different individuals or groups may not reach the same conclusions with regard to particular beliefs and practices.

As noted earlier, the religion of the immigrant group is transplanted from one context to another. In this sense, it is important to note that a religion is always embedded in a cultural environment. The dissociation of the ethnic and religious elements in the culture of a group should not be taken to mean that the religious culture evolving in the new cultural context is devoid of "non-supernatural" or secular elements. Indeed, it is likely to incorporate elements of the secular culture that the group members come to value as significant for the orientation of their lives in their adopted society.

A circumstance that may bring about such questioning is the religious, moral, and life-style pluralism of Western societies, which tends to entail regular encounters with people of different religious and cultural backgrounds. Perhaps even more critical would be regular contacts with people of the same religion but of a different ethnic background.

The interaction between immigrant parents and Canadian-born children can also make individuals aware that some beliefs or practices may not be essential elements in the religion. Such awareness may be more pronounced among women, and indeed, conceptions of gender roles and the related prescriptions are frequently sanctioned by the religion. The rejection of the inequality that often stems from these would be a force leading to the view that gender roles are defined by the ethnic and not by the religious culture.

It would be worthwhile examining the extent to which members of the mainstream society make a distinction between the religious and secular elements of the minority group's culture. Roy (2004, 10) states that "there is a constant confusion between Islam as a religion and 'Muslim culture' (if the expression makes sense, which I doubt)." The confusion may be found in popular culture, media reports of events, and public debates generally. This matter is clearly relevant for the evolution of views within the religious minority.

The blending of religious and ethno-cultural elements may also exist among members of mainstream religions. Implicitly or explicitly, elements that derive from their history as a people could be seen as integral to their religion. This phenomenon is especially apparent in the case of religions that became state religions at some point in history and in instances of political conflict between religious groups. For example, the blending of religious and ethnic factors is evident in the communal groups of Northern Ireland and in the two Canadian linguistic communities. Thus, the same question can be raised: is there a process of dissociation taking place in mainstream society as well as among members of religious minorities? This question is explored further in chapter 8.

The progressive dissociation of religion and ethnicity is an important element of integration into a new social and cultural environment. But there are other facets of the newcomer's religion and religiosity that evolve with time and generations. The fact of recognizing that one's religion is distinct from one's ethnicity is likely to be accompanied by other changes in the way in which individuals relate to their religion: changes in one's attitudes, religious identification, and participation. This is the subject of the following chapter.

4

Changes in Religious Attitudes and Practices

In their attempts to fit into the new social and institutional environment, immigrants and, especially, members of the second and subsequent generations tend to change in the ways they view and experience their religion. The role of religion in their lives evolves over time, an evolution that involves not only their personal lives and religious experience but also their relation with their community and the larger society.

Several authors have raised the matter of the evolution of ethnicity in the lives of individuals. Raising the question of the evolution of ethnicity presupposes that it is not entirely a primordial or ascribed feature of individual personalities that remains unchanged throughout their lives. Rather, it implies that it evolves in its content and in its relevance to their lives. The significance of ethnic identity and culture can become, to a degree, a matter of individual choice (McKay 1982). The same issue can be raised about religion: that is to say, the religion into which individuals are socialized in a childhood spent in a particular ethnic community may be abandoned or, if retained, can be so with a significantly modified set of beliefs and practices. In other words, religious affiliation and practice can become a matter of personal choice (Hammond and Warner 1993, 57, 66).

As noted above, religious commitment or religiosity can be expressed in different ways: through belief, practice, experience, knowledge, and everyday life. The evolution over time and generations can take place in one or more of these dimensions among members of majority and minority religious groups.

Several circumstances can impinge on the religiosity of new-comers and their descendants. The very fact of being an immigrant or a refugee may heighten the awareness of one's religion. Before emigration, the religious and cultural identity could be taken for granted. The transplantation may make newcomers less likely to abandon their religion and more likely to "demonstrate their adherence to it in a more self-conscious way than they were accustomed to doing" in the country of origin (McGown 1999, 95).

Features of the mainstream socio-cultural environment also affect the immigrants' relationship to their religion. The encounter with a highly individualistic and secular culture that is nevertheless informed deeply by a religious tradition alien to them (that is, Christianity) may provoke a crisis of identity that involves uncertainty as to what is expected of them. In such a situation, their identity and culture can no longer be taken for granted. They are more or less forced to reconsider their relationship with their own religion (McGown 1999, 97).

Western societies have themselves evolved considerably – and are still evolving – with regard to religious and moral attitudes and behaviour. Pluralism is a significant characteristic of these societies. There are a number of values and norms about which there is relatively little consensus and, as a result, considerable public debate. With regard to religion itself, a manifestation of pluralism is the increasingly accepted view that "all religions have elements of truth." In a relatively recent survey in the United States, 78 per cent agreed with that statement while only 17 per cent said that "their religion is the only true religion" (*Christian Century* 2002). No Canadian data could be found on this specific topic. However, such a distribution is likely to be the same in Canada, if not more accentuated.

Moreover, secularization has been progressing in Western societies for a number of decades. Secularization may refer to the separation of church and public institutions or to the religious neutrality of these institutions. Such a separation can be partial or complete. For the purposes of this discussion, secularization refers to the extent and modalities of individual attitudes and behaviour. It can be seen as a process by which religion "ceases to be at the center of human life, even though people still consider themselves believers" (Roy 2004, quoted in Gray 2008, 87). As a result, its personal and social significance can be reduced. In a related way, it can be seen as "a process whereby that which had been explained and understood in religious terms comes to be understood without reference to the divine and metaphysical" (Gitelman 2009, 304).[1]

Of course, secularization may not be taking place at the same pace and in the same way in all segments of a society, or it may not be taking place at all in some of them. In fact, in some socio-cultural milieux, the opposite may be the case. The importance of religion for individuals is intensified, and there is "de-secularization" in the sense that religion acquires a renewed and redefined significance more compatible with the changing experience of individuals. However, to the extent that secularization characterizes the culture of the particular segment of the receiving society into which new-comers settle, it can be expected that it will affect their religious attitudes and behaviour over time and generations.

One manifestation of the waning social significance of religion has been a decline in religious affiliation and practice. In Canada, the percentage of survey respondents who say they have no religion increased from less than 1 per cent in 1961 to 12 per cent in 1991 and to 19 per cent in 2004. As could be expected, the decline is related to age: in 2004, the proportion with no religious affiliation was only 8 per cent among those aged 60 and over, compared to 30 per cent among those aged 15 to 29 years. "At least monthly" religious service attendance also declined, from 41 per cent in 1985 to 32 per cent in 2004. In addition, the percentage declaring a religious affiliation but who do not attend religious services increased from 20 to 27 between 1985 and 2004.

Nevertheless, there are many who emphasize the subjective dimension of religious involvement: about 75 per cent of Canadians claim that spirituality is important to them, about half offering highly individualistic and subjective ideas of spirituality. The rest refer to spirituality in fairly traditional terms (Bibby 2004, 32, 86). A significant finding from the Ethnic Diversity Survey is that many Canadians who seldom or never attend services nevertheless engage in personal religious practices: 37 per cent do so every week. And even though such weekly practices are less frequent among the young than among older Canadians, they are still quite high among both groups: 27 per cent in the 15-to-29 age category compared to 45 per cent among those 60 years and over (Clark and Schellenberg, 2006: 4).

There is also a factor in the ethno-religious communities that facilitate religious acculturation, namely the fact that minority communities do not and cannot control the sources of social capital available to their members, especially after a number of years and generations in the new society. Drawing from Coleman (1988 1990), Portes and Sensenbrenner (1993), and Putnam (1993), we can posit that the following conditions give individuals access to social capital.

• Belonging to a group or social network in which there are norms of social obligation. People can then count on other members to respond to their *expectations for help or support*. The norms of obligation are based on value imperatives that prompt individuals to forgo self-interest and act in the interest of the collectivity.
• Finding others with whom they can engage in mutually beneficial transactions, whether these are instrumental or socio-emotional. Exchanges can consist of material assistance, information, approval and socio-emotional support. *Expectations in such exchanges are based on a common interest* in maintaining exchange relationships. Reciprocity and fairness are essential for transactions to be mutually beneficial.
• Having bounded solidarity or a community of fate. This derives from membership in a group or a social network whose members, in the face of similar problems or opportunities, realize that acting together can be advantageous. In this case, *social expectations are based on the fact everyone is in the*

same boat. Such a phenomenon may occur among immigrants who face problems of adaptation to new social and organizational environments with limited information and financial resources or among members of minorities who encounter rejection, hostility, or discrimination.

The hypothesis is that over time, new immigrants and especially their descendants enter progressively into relationships outside their own ethno-religious community for mutual support and exchange. The communities of interest to which they belong are located less and less within the boundaries of their own communities. Out-group relationships formed for various individual and family purposes (for example, work, education, recreation, or membership in community associations) tend to weaken the influence of in-group associations and organizations, including the religious. The community and its institutions lose whatever "moral monopoly"[2] they had in the initial phase of transplantation and integration.

A loss of "moral monopoly" means that the social organization of the community – including its religious organizations – together with the increased involvement of its members in the larger society, are such that the community is less and less able to impose conformity to its norms and role specifications (Boldt 1978, 360). In other words, the "structural tightness" of the community is a feature of social organization that pertains to the character of the social relations in the community. Specifically, it refers to "that particular dimension of relatedness suggested by ... the term 'tightness' [namely,] to the degree to which role expectations are 'imposed and received' as opposed to 'proposed and interpreted'" (Boldt 1978, 354).

As a result, individual role behaviour is less and less subject to surveillance by others in the religious community. And to the extent that this is the case, there will be opportunities for individuals to improvise on or deviate from the community's norms and specifications with impunity. In other words, they become more autonomous in the sense that they are more able or have more opportunities to pursue alternative courses of action. Role relationships within and outside of the community's social boundaries bring about a multiplicity of role expectations that may conflict with one another. Such a situation can have a paralyzing effect on the individual, but it can also "enhance accessibility to alternate courses of action" (Boldt, 1978, 355).[3]

This progressive evolution will tend to occur provided that there are no obstacles or barriers to the formation of ties of support, exchange, and solidarity across ethno-religious ands especially racial lines. Social marginality, as noted above, may result in a retreat into the ethno-religious community.

Three general questions concerning the evolution of the role of religion in the in the lives of individuals are examined in this chapter: (1) Are religious identification and practice persisting or declining? (2) Do members of religious minorities convert to one or another of the mainstream Christian religions? (3) Is religion becoming individualized? (4) Is there an evolution in the direction of "symbolic religiosity"?

MAINTENANCE OR DECLINE OF RELIGIOUS IDENTIFICATION AND PRACTICE?

To the extent that a decline of religion as a basis of social identity and affiliation among members of ethnic minorities takes place, it can be considered as part of the process of progressive acculturation. This has taken place among earlier cohorts of immigrants and especially their descendants. A decline can occur in both ethnic and non-ethnic church affiliation and practice.

In a Canada-wide study carried out in 1976 among ten ethnic minorities,[4] Reitz found that ethnic-church affiliation[5] had declined to 13 per cent among third-generation respondents from 57 per cent among adult immigrants. It had already declined to 24 per cent by the second generation (Reitz 1980, 131).

A relatively recent study among Sikhs in Vancouver also found significant changes across generations (Nayar 2004). "The first generation approaches religion as a set of normative structures that touch on all aspects of human behaviour and life. Religious tradition is understood as laying down norms for the whole of life, from the social domain to the spiritual" (128). Among the third generation, however, the tendency is not to take the tradition as a given but to ask questions about scriptures and Sikh religious history. Having absorbed the modern values of personal choice and self-orientation, they are less likely to accept the tradition passed through the generations (141). They tend to seek the essence of their religion and its spiritual aspects beyond its concrete forms and, more often than not, to distance themselves from religion as an institution (151).

O'Connell (2000, 201) quotes two unpublished surveys of the religious practices of small samples of Sikh respondents in the Toronto area. Both report more involvement in private religious practice by the grandparent generation than by the parent generation and least by the generation of children born in Canada.

Recent surveys show that immigrants and Canadian-born respondents have somewhat different religious profiles (Clark and Schellenberg 2006; Valpy and Friesen 2010). Immigrants are more likely to declare that religion is highly important to them: 55 and 57 per cent among those immigrated before 1982 and between 1982 and 2001, respectively, compared to 40 per cent among Canadian-born respondents. They are more likely to engage in private practices (50 compared to 40 per cent). In addition, the percentage declaring a religious affiliation but who do not attend religious services did not change among immigrants between 1985 and 2004 (whereas, as noted above, it decreased among the Canadian-born during that period). On a religious index combining affiliation, attendance, personal practices, and importance of religion, 40 per cent of immigrants scored "high" as compared to 26 per cent of Canadian-born respondents.

However, these overall results do not capture the possible variations within and among immigrant communities. Such variations do exist. For example, a 2002 survey found that the percentage who are the most likely to be religious varies between 21 and 65. It is highest among immigrants from Southern Asia, Southeast Asia, Central and South America, the Caribbean, and Africa, who are more likely to be highly religious (from 50 to 65 per cent) than those from West Central Asia, the Middle East, and Eastern Asia (from 21 to 33 per cent). The percentage is also low among immigrants from Europe and the United States.

A study in the National Capital Region carried out in the early 1990s assessed levels of religious commitment among a sample of 152 Muslim respondents from a community that is almost 90 per cent immigrant. The survey showed that approximately half reported a strong sense of Islamic identity based on their own perception with regard to the five pillars of Islam, about one-third showed a moderate level, and about one-fifth could be classified as "non-committed" (Yousif 1993, 51–2). Not surprisingly, the distribution of respondents is about the same when asked if they consider the possibility of losing their Islamic identity and faith as a problem: this is a serious problem for one-half, a moderate problem for one-fifth, and not a problem for about one-third. In other words, the sample is roughly divided in half between those with a strong commitment and those with a moderate or no commitment.

Using longitudinal data among immigrants to Canada in 2001,[6] Connor (2009, 162) found that religious participation declines marginally over each of three time periods during the first five years in Canada.[7] It should be mentioned, however, that the question asked about the respondents' "group participation in a variety of organizations, including religious, ethnic, cultural, and community groups." The fact that only about 15 per cent said they participated in a religious group may be due to the fact many did not include churches, mosques, or temples among "the variety of organizations" in which they participate. In may also explain the high level of participation among those who would have included churches, temples, and mosques in their response (95 per cent six months after migration, 92 per cent after two years, and 89 per cent after five years in the country), as well as the fact that religious volunteerism increased significantly during that period, from 39 to 64 per cent.

There may have been an ambiguity due to the wording of the question. Indeed, in his analysis of survey data from a Quebec sample (N = 1,000)[8] in which the question asked dealt specifically with religious participation ("Since your arrival to Quebec, how often have you gone to a temple or church?"), Connor (2008, 248) found that religious participation dropped from 48 to 40 per cent after three years in the country. These percentages are much higher than the 15 per cent observed in the Canada-wide sample, a difference that reflects, in part, a difference in the wording of the question in the two sets of data. The Quebec sample also revealed a drop in religious attendance after immigration to Quebec, from 56 to 48 per cent one year after immigration (Connor 2008, 249). This is not surprising since behaviour tends to be less constrained by tradition and prohibitions in the new social context (Kepel 1997, 49–50). The high level of secularization in Quebec noted by Connor (2008) could be an element contributing to the freedom of choice available to new immigrants.

A large-scale survey conducted across Canada[9] in 2002 on the importance attached to religion, participation in religious activities, attendance at religious services,[10] and private prayer show that, in general, there is a lower level of religiosity on all three measures among Judeo-Christians than among Muslims and members of other Eastern religions (including Sikhs, Hindus, and Buddhists).[11]

As can be seen from table 2, the patterns of differences in religious practices between adherents of the major religious categories are not clear-cut. Muslims are just as likely to say they do not engage in public worship at all as to say that they do on a weekly basis. This is the case for Judeo-Christians as well, but they are also more likely than Muslims to attend public services only occasionally. The three groups are very similar in frequency of private worship or prayer.

However, groups differ in their demographic characteristics, such as their immigration status (recent or earlier immigrant and Canadian-born), visible-minority status, gender, age, level of education, and household income. When these characteristics of group members are taken into account (the column "with controls" in the table), the differences not only disappear but, in the case of Muslims (though not of the other non-Judeo-Christian groups), are reversed: Muslims attach significantly less importance to

Table 2
Importance attached to religion and indicators of religious practice, by religious affiliation

Religious affiliation	Importance attached to religion		Participation in religious services		Private worship		
	Observed	with controls	Observed	with controls	Observed	with controls	N
Judeo-Christian	3.53	3.51	3.03	3.06	3.62	3.63	30,325
Muslim	4.22	3.29	2.96	2.38	3.98	2.96	813
Other and Eastern	4.21	4.19	3.35	3.15	4.01	4.64	1,794

Source: Based on data from the 2002 Statistics Canada Ethnic Diversity Survey as presented in Reitz et al. (2009). Statistical analysis by Mai Phan.

Note: $N = 41,666$. The numbers in the table are mean scores: respondents rated the importance of religion in their lives as not at all important, a little bit important, somewhat important, important and very important. They described the frequency of participation in religious activities with others as not at all, once or twice a year, at least three times a year, at least once a month or at least once a week. They also rated the frequency of religious prayer or private worship in that way. For each variable, the possible scores varied from 0 to 5; the numbers in the table are the average scores for each of the three categories of respondent.

religion, participate less often in religious services, and engage less often in private worship or prayer than adherents of Judeo-Christian, "Other" and Eastern religions.

But what is the significance of these patterns? For instance, the decline in religious practice and affiliation may not signify a decline in the importance of religion itself but of the ways it has been (and continues to be) institutionalized (for example, the forms, rituals, and symbols with which it had been traditionally practised) and of the array of religious prescriptions and proscriptions. Individuals drift away from institutions that have lost (or are losing) meaning for them. They may abandon formal religious practice and search for other forms or avenues of religious expression, such as membership in informal groups, religious voluntarism, and private prayer or meditation. Different manifestations of the importance of religion for individuals need to be taken into consideration.

As indicated earlier, there are variations among individual within and between religious groups in their religious concepts and in the ways in which they evaluate and apply the values and norms of their religion. The study by Maynard et al. (2001, 71–2) mentioned earlier showed that such variations are associated with an individual's concept of God. Specifically, the latter was found to be correlated with the importance attached to religion and spirituality as well as to religious participation (see also Bader and Froese 2005).[12] The variations may also mean that "the definition of religion is widened to include questions about individual and social health ... the future of the planet" and other issues not usually associated with religious orthodoxy (Davie 1993, 17, 26). Some of these issues are explored in the following sections.

CONVERSIONS AND INTER-RELIGIOUS MARRIAGES

One path followed by some, though relatively few, members of religious minorities is conversion to a mainstream Christian denomination. Partners in mixed marriages and the offspring of such marriages tend to adopt the religion of the majority if they retain a religious affiliation (Beyer 2005, 192). A study of Chinese-American students relates conversion to "openness" and "receptivity factors" (Hall 2006). A weakening of the traditional culture, for example, may render second-generation members of the community more open to a mainstream religion. Hall also notes that, unlike Christianity, Buddhism is not a proselytizing religion that makes a claim to the sole religious "truth." This "openness" in Buddhism may help explain why many parents did not mind their children being involved in Christian activities and attending Catholic schools. The perceived modernness of Christianity may also make it attractive to them. The "receptivity" factors mentioned above are the attitudes of the mainstream Christian churches, as shown, for example, in their offer of different forms of help in coping with the problems of daily life.

Individuals may convert for a number of reasons. It can be a strategy pursued by some members of minority groups seeking to integrate culturally, economically, and socially into the society (Nagata 1987; Lin 2009, 175). This has been observed, for instance, among middle-class Japanese and Chinese families in British Columbia. The Christian missions were attractive to them partly because of the educational, childcare, and recreational services that helped them to meet their economic and social needs (Knowles 1995, 71).

Form (2000, 312) also observed that conversion (to Protestantism) tends to occur among those most eager to Americanize and become upwardly mobile. For Hindu youth in Trinidad, conversion to Christianity opened opportunities for social and professional mobility, most notably in education (Vertovec 1990, 230). For many Hmong in Canada, "religious change is an acculturative mechanism bridging traditional values and practices with Western ones and encouraging attitudes and behaviour more consonant with western values and practices" (Winland 1992, 104). However, Winland also points out that religious conversion is not necessarily an instrumental strategy but may be the result of an individual's deliberate attempt to make sense of his or her religious beliefs by confronting them with those of another religion (105). Thus, conversion may be a process in which immigrants are consciously looking for meaning in their new religious environment. It may not be instrumental, but it is nevertheless part of the process of adapting to a new sociocultural environment.

There are a number of inter-religious unions[13] in Canada. An analysis of the Ethnic Diversity Survey revealed that the proportion of the population that is part of an inter-religious couple is 9 per cent among Muslims and Hindus, 19 per cent among Buddhists, 9 per cent among Hindus, 17 per cent among Jews, 3 per cent among Sikhs, and 27 per cent among "other Eastern religions." The likelihood of inter-religious marriages is greater if there are few co-religionists in the community. In addition, if the parents' union is inter-religious, their adult children's marriages are more likely to be inter-religious (Clark 2006, 18, 20, 21).

Inter-religious marriages may bring about a conversion of one of the partner to the other's religion. If a conversion does take place, it may reinforce the attachment to one's religion if one's partner adopts it; but it may result in a decreased involvement in it if the partner does not. The influence of intermarriage on religious attitudes and behaviour needs empirical exploration. It is not a large-scale phenomenon, but it is not negligible and may increase with time and generations in the receiving society.

INDIVIDUALIZATION OF RELIGION

The individualization or privatization of religion may take place with regard to doctrine and related moral imperatives and to the manner of participation, the emphasis being put on the personal rather than the institutional. In an individualized religion the emphasis is on personal choice and inner feelings of truth. "The approach to religious truth changes – away from any objective grounds on which it must be judged, to a more subjective, more instrumental understanding of what it does for the believer, and how it can do what it does most efficiently" (Roof 1993, 195).

At this point, a comment on terminology should be made. The research literature uses the terms "individualization" and "privatization," as well as "interiorized religion." Sometimes these terms are used interchangeably, but sometimes they are given somewhat different meanings. In an *individualized* religion, individuals make choices according to what is compatible with their own life circumstances and experience. *Privatized* religion is one that is practised in the private as opposed to the public sphere. And an *interiorized* religion emphasizes the spiritual element of religion as opposed to its ritualistic and devotional practices. Both conceptual clarifications and empirical verifications are needed in this connection.

Whatever term is used, the process involved does not necessarily mean a rupture with the institution, but it usually involves a different emphasis. Here the distinction between "religion" and "spirituality" is relevant. As explained by Roof (2003, 138), religion refers to such elements as scripture, ritual, beliefs, practices, moral codes, and institutions, whereas spirituality refers to the quest for meaning, self-fulfillment, and individual growth.

The individualization of religion may lead to a "religion à la carte" and the freedom to choose within the institution what the individual feels provides a set of meanings compatible with his or own life circumstances and experience (Bibby 1987, chap. 4). The commitment is not to the institution but to a search for what is helpful for developing one's potential and defining one's relationships to others and to society. Bibby (1987, 81) suggests that the shift in religious style that has progressively taken place for several decades involves a movement from religious commitment to religious consumption. This involves the selection of ritual obligations and an adaptation of regulations to the circumstances in which individuals find themselves.

Another way of characterizing the trend would be to say that religion remains significant for the *personal* identity of individuals but not so much for their *social* identity. Indeed, *personal identity* is "constructed by the person not in relation to a community and its culture but in relation to the self and its projects" (Hewitt 1989, 179). The frame of reference for the definition of one's *social identity* is "a community, which is the source of a generalized sense of place or perspective, and a culture, which defines that community and provides purpose for the individual's life" (170). Of course, it is not that individuals come to have no social identity; rather, it is that other communities and related cultures become more central than the religious in defining social identity.

It seems that this phenomenon is also taking place among members of both mainstream and of minority religions. Among the latter, it occurs especially in the second and subsequent generations. Eid (2003, 50) observed that among second-generation Arab Canadians (both Christian and Muslim), "religious identity is significantly more developed at the subjective, as opposed to the objective level." Specifically, he found (2007, 112, 114) that about 59 per cent never or rarely attend religious services or attend them on religious holidays only. In contrast, 71 per cent pray once a day or more or once a week. In other words, affiliation with a religion may be nominal, and participation in a church, synagogue, or temple may cease or become sporadic, but there may still be a set of beliefs and practices that matter to individuals. Another study of Canadian second-generation youth also reveals a process of individualization. "Irrespective of which religious background one is considering, the approach to religion of this population is for the most part highly individualistic, meaning that they base the extent and content of their religious involvement or lack thereof on their own decisions, their own researches, their own experience" (Beyer 2008, 30).

Both Eid (2007, 114–15) and Beyer (2008, 31) point out that, in their shift toward individual responsibility, the participants in the study are following the dominant pattern of the overall Canadian population. This phenomenon is part of the process of acculturation. Eid's (2007, 105) findings show that whereas 77 per cent of the young respondents consider their parents' religious identity to either "very strong" or "strong," only 15 per cent describe their own as such.

The privatization of religion has also been observed among Muslims in Europe and the United States. Religious practice is freed "from the social conventions and standards of Islam as practiced in officially Muslim countries ... To be Muslim in Europe or the United States means to lose one's relationship to Islam as a cultural and social *fait accompli*, and instead to open it up to questioning and individual choice" (Cesari 2004a, 45). The "believer-consumer" behaviour mentioned above has also been observed among Muslims in European countries (Cesari 2004b, 151).[14]

The "master" frame of reference for the social identity and social relations of some individuals may progressively become other than ethnic or religious. Although being anchored in a community is deemed to be important for the development of the individual, it should not be assumed that the ethnic group or the religious community are the *only* communities that can play this role (Gross 1993). They may be central in a person's childhood, but as an adult, he or she is also socialized into professional, industrial, ideological, or political communities. Ethnicity or religion does not necessarily become insignificant, but it may become only one of the bases – and possibly a minor one at that – in the definition of one's social identity and affiliations, rather than the master frame of reference.

One reason for such a development is that the ethnic group or religious community may be experienced as a source of social constraint as well as social support. People "are drawn toward the comfort and security of community. But people are also drawn toward the freedom of modern society, toward the construction of selves whose sphere is the society, and its more abstract and dispersed communities. One reason is that organic communities make claims upon individuals. They confer a sense of place and purpose, but they also impose obligations" (Hewitt 1989, 115).

Individuals may wish to avoid social obligations, but it could be argued that more often, privatization or individual choice means that individuals wish to choose which obligations they want to impose upon themselves. In a survey (N = 2,014) carried out in Canada in 1997, almost all respondents felt some obligation to help others. However, the sense of social obligation was not directed primarily toward one's own ethnic, cultural, or racial group: 18 per cent declared a *strong* sense of obligation to help people of the same ethnic, cultural, or racial background, compared to 30 per cent who felt a strong obligation to help people "in the same boat as I am in life," and 35 per cent to help anyone in need. The percentages expressing a weak sense of obligation were 40, 21, and 14 respectively (the remaining respondents expressed a moderate sense of obligation). In other words, the sense of obligation tended to be more universalistic than particularistic – an orientation associated with the acceptance of diversity[15] (Breton et al. 2004, chap. 9).

However, an earlier study (N = 2,338) carried out in 1978–9 found that the feeling of obligation towards members of one's own ethnic group varies considerably with ethnic group,[16] with the type of help involved,[17] and with the number of generations one's family has been in Canada. It is the highest among Jews with regard to helping a group member find a job, marrying within the group, and supporting group needs and causes (Isajiw 1990, 78–9).

The evidence shows that individuals change in the process of integrating into a new socio-cultural environment. There are of course variations among individuals, religious groups, and sub-groups – variations that need further empirical investigation. For example, a study carried out in 2002 found that, in Canada, the degree of religiosity[18] varies considerably among immigrants from different regions of the world. The proportion with a high score on the index of religiosity varied from 65 per cent among South Asians to 21 per cent among East Asians. Small percentages were also found among the Canadian-born (26 per cent) and among immigrants from European and Northern Europe (24 per cent) (Clark and Schellenberg, 2006, 8).[19]

The cultural milieu in which integration takes place is characterized by modernity. In such a milieu, membership in any one collectivity or group does not automatically imply identification with or participation in it. The multiplicity of possible social connections implies the possibility of choice and of multiple identifications and attachments. In other words, membership tends to be voluntary rather than simply ascribed at birth.

A factor that needs to be examined is that the change in the social frame of reference may well have begun in the country of origin. The earlier experience and cultural traditions of immigrants may be quite different from what the receiving society assumes them to be. This was suggested by Smith (1971, 215), who argued that "older Americans assumed that the faith of the newcomers stemmed from blind adherence to village or ethnic traditions which were irrelevant in a commercial or industrial society – traditions imposed and maintained by an authoritarian church hierarchy." He proposed a diametrically opposed framework of interpretation, namely, that "village religion in the 'Old World' was by no means a bastion of social and ecclesiastical privilege. On the contrary, laymen often played key roles in both local and regional religious affairs and expected priests, bishops, and rabbis to support lay social and political interests."

This may be the case for immigrants from countries such as India, China, Pakistan, and Iran. A recent column in a Canadian newspaper quoted an Iranian philosopher, Daryush Shayegan, who said it was inevitable that Islamic fervour would be transformed into politics and the secularism of politics would then destroy the sacred nature of Islam, its own religious base. This is a metamorphosis that is under way. It is not, he argues, that Iranians are becoming anti-religious, but that they want more of a private religion than a public one (Saunders 2007, F3). Those who leave countries such as Iran and Pakistan may well be among those who are the most advanced in that metamorphosis. They may have begun in their country of origin the shift from orthodox institutional practices to a privatized religiosity.[20]

The privatization of religion does not mean that religion is ceasing to be important for individuals. Rather, it means that it is important in a different way. People's religious involvement may take place less and less through formally organized rituals and more and more through practices carried out privately or in small informal groups. Such an orientation may also manifest itself in an exploration of different religious traditions and in an emphasis on "spirituality" rather than conventional religious practice.

EVOLUTION IN THE DIRECTION OF "SYMBOLIC RELIGIOSITY"?

Several authors have suggested that both ethnic and religious identities become progressively "symbolic" with time in the host society. The terms used differ: "symbolic ethnicity" is used by Gans (1979, 1994), "sidestream ethnicity" by Fishman (1985), and "affective ethnicity" by Weinfeld (1981). But these expressions all seem to refer to the same phenomenon. "Symbolic ethnicity – and the consumption and other use of ethnic symbols – is intended mainly for the purpose of feeling or being identified with a particular ethnicity, but without either participating in an existing ethnic organization (formal or informal) or practicing an ongoing ethnic culture" (Gans 1994, 578). Ethnic affiliation no longer structures people's lives and social relationships, and its role is no longer to help or hinder the achieving of success in the society but simply to provide "roots" (Gans 1979; Warner and Wittner 1998, 61).

Gans (1994, 585–6) has suggested that this is also the case with religion. The hypothesis is that there is a shift towards symbolic religiosity, that is, towards the "consumption of religious symbols apart from regular participation in a religious culture or in religious organizations, other than for purely secular purposes." Religious (and ethnic) affiliations impose little obligations on individuals, specify few if any role expectations, and become progressively unrelated to the formation of their social networks. Whereas in traditional societies religion was co-extensive with social life, that is no longer the case in modern societies, in which the church is a voluntary association. "The church is not simultaneously a gathering of kin, neighbours, fellow workers, and leisure-time friends but rather a separate activity, expressing another meaning. The church may be an important source of identity, but it is only one of several segmented relationships" (Hammond 1992, 2–6).

It is important to note that the "symbolic religiosity" hypothesis may not be equally valid in all religious collectivities or in all their different segments. For instance, it may not apply, or may apply less, to members of groups that are ethnically or racially different from the mainstream population and that may experience various forms of social exclusion that leads them to seek refuge in their religious identity.

A case study of American Jews offers an instance where the "symbolic religiosity" hypothesis does not apply. In that study, Kivisto and Nefzger (1993, 7–8) found a strong correlation between the importance attached to being a Jew and membership in temple or synagogue. Among those respondents, religious identification is not only symbolic; it also associated with membership in a religious institution. This may be because for Jews there is a fusion of religion and ethnicity, in contrast with most other groups of European origin. The authors also note variations among Jewish sub-communities depending on the availability of easily accessible institutions in the community, which in turn depends on its size and institutional completeness.

A study of second-generation Turkish youth in the Netherlands may also help specify some of the conditions under which the "symbolic-religiosity" hypothesis applies. Respondents in that study were classified into five attitudinal categories:

(a) incontestable acceptance of a traditional dualistic world view (51 per cent), (b) reserved acceptance (11 per cent), (c) ambivalent attitude (18 per cent), (d) positive attitude toward religion without acceptance of the concrete representations of the supernatural (7 per cent), and (e) rejection of ideological collective representations (13 per cent). The authors note that this "pattern suggests that the five attitudinal types represent a hierarchy of increasing secularization" (van der Lans and Rooijackers 1994, 118–19).

However, it was also found that the five attitudinal types do not differ much from one other with regard to the observance of certain obligations, such as the daily prayer (which is generally the least observed). This shows that rejection of traditional religious ideas can accompany a certain degree of religious observance. And the fact that the great majority of respondents accept to some extent the traditional collective religious representations suggests a strong degree of social integration. The adherence to traditional religious representations can serve a protective function, and abandoning these will diminish the individual's integration into the community and may have anomic effects (van der Lans and Rooijackers 1994, 126). Again, as noted by Kivisto and Nefzger, this suggests a certain fusion between ethnicity and religion that combines adherence to religious beliefs and social integration into the community through religious or secular activities and relationships.

The "symbolic" shift may take place for both ethnicity and religion, but it may not take place sooner and faster for one than for the other. Gans (1994, 581) suggests that people who lose interest in religion may drop it more quickly than the secular parts of their ethnicity. However, it could also be hypothesized that ethnicity disappears faster than a group's religion. This would be so because ethnic groups tend to be less well organized than religious groups, their social organization consisting primarily of informal groups. Conversely, religious groups are usually more formally organized. Informal groups play interstitial roles. "Furthermore, the speed of acculturation in the two domains might be affected by the fact that in America, religiosity can be a truly private activity which requires no affiliation in a way that ethnicity, including the symbolic variety, cannot be."

VARIATIONS BETWEEN AND WITHIN RELIGIOUS COLLECTIVITIES

The extent and patterns of change in religious attitudes and behaviour may vary among the different religious minorities, as well as within them. For example, Cesari (2004a, 46ff) identifies three types of Muslims as far as practice is concerned: (a) those who practise a private version of their faith; (b) non-practising Muslims who nevertheless identify with the religion in the sense that they adhere to its moral and humanistic values, particularly the ideal of voluntarism; and (c) fundamentalists who embrace a totalizing version of communal Islam.

Different social categories of people may "express their religion in different ways or along different dimensions." For example, "lower-class people are more likely to pray in private, to believe in the doctrines of their faith, and to have intense religious experiences. But the upper classes display greater religious commitment when it comes to church membership, church attendance, and all other aspects of the ritual dimension (Stark and Bainbridge 1985, 10–11; see also Stark 1972). Such variations need to be explored empirically.

Religion offers intangible and tangible rewards to its adherents. "Thus people can gain a variety of rewards from religious commitment. They can earn a living from religion. Religions offer different types of rewards to their members: human companionship, status as an upright person of good character, leisure and recreational activity, opportunities for marriage, courtship, and business contacts" (Stark and Bainbridge 1985, 11). Such intangible and tangible rewards may not be equally attractive or meaningful for all social and cultural groups. There are variations in this regard by age, gender, social class, occupation, community of residence, and ethno-cultural and religious group.

A worthwhile line of research in this connection is suggested by the classification of religious "niches" (within a religion) according to the strictness of their beliefs, values, and norms (Stark and Finke 2000). The following is a possible typology of strictness: ultra-strict, strict, moderate-conservative, liberal, and ultra-liberal. "The liberal niche includes those who are prepared to accept the liberal values that prevail in modern society; the ultraliberal niche includes "modernists" who enthusiastically embrace these liberal values and are willing to give them a religious sanction ... By contrast those in the strict niche see the prevailing liberal values as negative and dangerous, and those in the ultrastrict niche require absolute separation from these values, which are perceived as truly perverse and even demonic. Those in the moderate-conservative niche do not utterly reject modern values but feel free to reinterpret them on the basis of religious tradition while in turn reinterpreting religion to make it relevant to the modern world" (Introvigne 2005, 5).

Research on how members of minority religions vary in their orientation to religious strictness and, especially, how they evolve in this regard over time in Canada and over generations could throw light on the process of acculturation and integration into the receiving society. A general hypothesis would be that, with time, those who are at the strictness extreme would move progressively toward the moderate-conservative "centre" since the lifestyle and moral "costs" to be assumed would progressively come to be seen as too heavy or as inappropriate in the new cultural context. These costs could be symbolic, such as a world view that is not compatible with the main elements of the mainstream culture, or practical, such as a constraining lifestyle and limited social relations. Religious organizations would also tend to move toward the centre so as not to lose too many members and not to provoke opposition from the larger society.[21]

CONCLUSION

Certain features of the new cultural context, such as secularization and religious pluralism, can lead members of minorities to question their religious allegiances, beliefs, moral values, and participation. The process of integration may bring about the perception of a lack of fit between the traditional religion and the new cultural milieu. This perception may result in creative adaptations of religious prescriptions, a weakening of religion as a basis of social identity and community attachments, or a decline in religious involvement and practice. Another factor that may account for changes in religious attitudes and practices is the increased choices available to individuals. This is partly due to the cultural and social pluralism in the larger society. It is also due to the progressively declining capacity of the minority community to impose conformity to its norms and role specifications. To the extent that social integration is taking place, individuals are increasingly susceptible to pressures from groups other than their religious community.

The evidence suggests that the patterns that emerge over time and generations with regard to religiosity in religious minorities tend progressively to mirror those that have come to prevail in recent decades in the mainstream society. As a result, the same variations in religiosity and practices would eventually be observed among minorities as among members of the larger society.

The social and cultural context in which integration that takes place does not have an influence only on individuals; it also affects the religious organizations of the community. The next two chapters examine two sets of processes involved in their progressive integration into the adopted society. The first has to do with the changing role that community religious organizations play in relation to their members; the second concerns their internal transformations, both doctrinal and organizational.

PART THREE

The Evolution of Minority Religious Organizations

Changing social circumstances and the evolution of individual members of the community have implications for the institutions of minority groups, including their churches and religious organizations. These institutions are confronted, not only with new demands on the part of their members, but also with the potential loss of members. As members become acculturated, lose fluency in their heritage language, and have more choices in their social affiliations, the appeal of ethnic organizations, including churches and religious organizations, becomes gradually weaker, unless, as indicated above, the members experience hostility, economic discrimination, and social exclusion from the mainstream society. But if integration is progressively taking place, minority-group leaders have to deal with the organizations in the larger society that may attract their members or potential members. If the minority religious organizations are unable to meet this challenge, they will eventually cease to exist, at least as ethnic religious organizations.

Several studies have examined how different religious organizations respond to such challenges, especially those that arise with the emergence of the second generation. Generally, it has been observed that in order to keep their acculturated members, ethnic religious institutions transform themselves in such a way that they themselves become progressively acculturated or "de-ethnicized."

In particular, in order to remain relevant, they develop programs and activities that will facilitate the integration of their members – as explicit strategies or as practical arrangements suggested by members. They may also reinterpret doctrines and moral specifications or modify rituals and practices in order to adapt better to the new cultural environment and to the changing experiences of their adherents. The next two chapters examine the role of religious organizations as agents of acculturation and integration and their internal transformation.

5

Religious Organizations as Agents of Acculturation and Integration

An organizational response to these changes and challenges has been to move progressively away from immigrant adaptation services and the maintenance of ethno-cultural traditions and identity and to focus on the acculturation of their members and their integration into the larger society. In addition to their religious functions, religious organizations become more and more concerned with functions that could facilitate the full participation of their members in the host society (White 1994; Doomernik 1995; Bankston and Zhou 1996).

There are at least four ways in which religion and churches can have an influence on the social integration of immigrants and ethnic minorities. They can (a) provide practical services and social opportunities; (b) foster social and civic participation; (c) make available cultural tools to cope with the moral challenges encountered in the new cultural milieu; and (d) offer a paradigm by which the new society is defined by members of the minority.

PROVIDING SERVICES AND OPPORTUNITIES FOR SOCIAL MOBILITY AND SKILL DEVELOPMENT

A variety of practical services have been introduced by churches and religious organizations to facilitate the integration into the larger society. Several of these involve a broadening of the role of the clergy beyond the traditional one of ritual and scriptural expert. They include such services as computer and language courses, personal counselling, assistance in the preparation of income tax returns, and the establishment of a health-care centre with the help of doctors and nurses. The church can also act as a broker to connect church members with the bureaucratic institutions of the larger society. A group of professionals provide church members with counselling on immigration and naturalization, employment, housing, health care, social security, and education (Chafetz and Ebaugh 2002; Kim 1981). The importance of these kinds of church programs and services is underscored by the fact that they sometimes become occasions of inter-church competition for membership and prestige (Kim 1981, 202).

Different services may be provided to members of the first and the second generation. For example, as Korean communities make the transition from an immigrant community to an immigrant-ethnic community, the secular functions of Korean churches undergo changes. In the early stage of development, they provide new immigrants with fellowship and various services associated with immigrant adjustment. However, with time, what becomes more important is education in the Korean language and culture for second-generation children and opportunities for gains in social status for adult immigrants (Min 1992, 1371; Hurh and Kim 1990, 30–1).

Church-related activities may have a broad acculturation effect, as in the case of early German Catholics in Saskatchewan. The Catholic school they established seems to have been an instrument of linguistic assimilation from German to English. The members of the clergy and the laity who created the Catholic schools were more concerned with safeguarding their faith than their language (White 1994).

FOSTERING SOCIAL AND CIVIC PARTICIPATION

Religious (and civic) leaders can be active in promoting civic and political participation. Church-related organizations and activities can provide opportunities for the development of leadership and other skills relevant for effective involvement, not only in the community, but in the larger society as well (Foner and Alba 2008, 363–8; Eck 2001, 359–66). Foley and Hoge (2007, 153–60) studied the level of participation in several areas in a number of faith communities:[1] participation in the worship service, organizing community life, congregational governance, and training in civic skills and civic engagement. The latter included, among other activities, voter-registration drives, discussions of political issues, meetings to plan an assessment of community needs, citizenship classes, and discussions of race relations. Considerable variations were observed among the different communities, but generally the level of participation was not negligible.

The active encouragement of civic engagement in a democratic society can also be achieved by the promoting of a *selective-engagement* paradigm, discussed later, which emphasizes the importance of becoming involved in some social or political cause (Mattson 2003). For example, during the 2008 Canadian federal election, some mosque leaders got "involved to thwart usual apathy on election day ... by inviting local candidates to meet their congregations, and encouraging the ranks to evaluate their platform." They emphasized the idea that "you cannot be a caring citizen unless you vote" (Wallace 2008).

It will be seen later that the pursuit of recognition in the mainstream society also requires political mobilization in the community. Such an objective may be an incentive to become involved in the political life of the larger society. To a certain extent, it could raise the civic and political consciousness of community members and increase their sense that they can be active citizens in the society. The pursuit of recognition by the larger society, however, may be avoided by some members because it is seen as hindering rather than facilitating their integration into the mainstream.

PROVIDING TOOLS TO COPE
WITH "NEW" MORAL CHALLENGES

Parents and church leaders may realize that the culture of the larger society entails moral challenges, particularly for children and adolescents. Religion is then seen as providing a moral code to assist in meeting the challenge (Ajrouch 1999, 124). In a study of an American-Chinese community, it was observed that the main reason for involvement in the Chinese evangelical church (after moving to the United States) was to protect the children from the lax sexual standards and consumer-oriented culture of the surrounding society, including school violence, drug abuse, and teenage pregnancies. Thus, religion is seen as providing a solid foundation for coping with life in America (Chen 2006, 574; Zhou and Bankston 1998).

Religion can change relationships in a family undergoing the process of social integration, especially those between parents and children. Religion can reproduce traditions and maintain certain patterns of life, but it may also change inherited traditions. For example, as noted earlier, parents know that it is not possible to re-create the Confucian culture and life patterns in North America (Chen 2006, 580). Their dilemma is that, on the one hand, Confucian principles have lost their moral legitimacy in the family and on the other hand, they do not find that mainstream America offers attractive models for the family. In response, Taiwanese immigrants turn to the church for solutions. Immigrant parents abandon the Confucian language of indebtedness and obligation and adopt the moral language of Christian discipleship to achieve traditionally Confucian ends (Chen 2006, 583). The source of authority is not the parents themselves, but the Bible. Parents realize that it is no longer effective to use the language of filial piety and duty. Christianity frames the issues as personal choices: it is a personal choice to commit one's life to Christ. In this way, parents are able simultaneously to discipline their children and affirm the children's sense of personal freedom (590–1). Thus, in the process of negotiating Confucian traditions in American society, East Asian families transform these traditions. Through such adaptation, religion plays a role in creating new family patterns – less controlling and more egalitarian – that are consistent with the cultural patterns of the new environment.

Through the teaching of norms that affirm the legitimacy of what they consider desirable values in the adopted society, religious organizations can serve to integrate young people into the mainstream society (Bankston and Zhou 1996, 31). Wittingly or unwittingly, they perform a socializing function that can affect the acculturation of their members. It can be a significant socialization since it can legitimize some elements of the mainstream culture in the eyes of their adherents.

In their attempt to integrate and participate actively in a multicultural and multi-religious society, many new immigrants and their children are forced to reflect on their own values, ideas, and patterns of behaviour. They are confronted with issues concerning the situation of the young and the elderly; problems of education, employment, violence, and juvenile delinquency; the subjugation of girls and women; and the abuse of basic human rights (Naguib 2002, 172–3). Having to reflect on those issues may lead them to address problems within their own communities. The integration of newcomers brings about cultural challenges for the immigrant community and the receiving society. These require transformations in both communities. Such changes are facilitated if the organizational elites of both communities take an active role, not only in attempting to have the other side modify their attitudes and behaviour in regard to the changing circumstances, but also in promoting attitudinal and behavioural changes within their own communities. The paradigm through which the adopted society is defined is important in this connection.

OFFERING A PARADIGM THROUGH WHICH THE ADOPTED SOCIETY IS DEFINED

Religious organizations can also contribute to shaping the paradigm that the immigrant and second generations use to define and relate to the mainstream society. "In order to understand their role in America, Muslims need to define not only Islam but also America. Muslims need to place America in its proper theological and legal category so they can determine what kind of relationship is possible and desirable for them to have with this country" (Mattson 2003, 200). That is also applicable to other religious minorities. The argument is that responses to main-stream society will be partly a function of the paradigm used to define the critical features of that society. A paradigm of *resistance* is based on a view of the state and society as belligerent vis-à-vis one's religion or the country in which one's religion is dominant. A paradigm of "*embrace*" focuses on positive characteristics of the society and its culture, such as democracy, freedom, and equality. Finally, a third possibility is a paradigm of *selective engagement*. This is consistent with the paradigm of embrace, but it emphasizes the need to have a positive influence in the larger society or community by adopting various social and political causes, such as environmentalism, social justice, or higher levels of education.

Of course, the paradigms do not emerge in a cultural, social, and political vacuum. They emerge through exchanges, debates, and discussion among members of the groups who have different values and opinions about their society of adoption and how they should relate to it. In the host society paradigms also emerge that identify certain characteristics of the new groups and that affect the social and political responses to their presence, culture, and aspirations. An interesting empirical question concerns the role – if any – that mainstream and minority churches play in shaping the construction, interaction, and evolution of those paradigms.

An interesting illustration of such a role is revealed in a comparison of the paradigms used by the Catholic and the Evangelical Salvadoran churches in their efforts to assist immigrants. The Catholic congregations have a "communitarian ethic" in which the focus is on efforts by the collectivity to improve the immigrants' situation. This community approach led leaders and members to reach out to and unite a large and ethnically diverse membership – that is, immigrant Catholics of different cultural backgrounds.

In contrast, in the Evangelical congregations (usually founded by the new immigrants themselves), the focus is on individual salvation. "When asked if their church should seek solutions to social problems, Evangelicals in all three locations overwhelmingly answered negatively, as they did not readily see how such actions could be of more benefit than a conversion which guarantees not only salvation but also better people in general." This "focus on individual salvation leads efforts to bring the benefits of conversion to its smaller and more ethnically homogeneous flock" (Menjivar 2003, 29, 39).

A similar difference in orientation was observed in a comparative study of a Taiwanese immigrant Buddhist temple and an Evangelical Christian church in the United States (Chen 2002). The mission and institutionalized strategy of the Christian Evangelical church is defined by personal evangelism. Because evangelizing takes place largely through personal networks, this strategy leads to a focus on members of the same ethnic and racial group and limits interactions with those outside of the Chinese-speaking community. "Its most valuable resource for outreach, its members, is simultaneously an obstacle that hinders it from outreach beyond the ethnic immigrant community" (Chen 2002, 226).

In contrast, the theological orientation of the Buddhist Dharma Light Temple is a mission of charity, which is a radically different understanding of "salvation" than evangelical Christianity. "Buddhists regard the world and their present lives as a temporary realm where they work out their karmic debts and merits." The temple exists for its own adherents, but it does extend beyond its own community, the world being a place where individuals can work out their own salvation and that of others through good thoughts and deeds. "Just as the evangelical church becomes an institution of salvation through preaching the gospel, the Buddhist church is so by giving its devotees the opportunity to do good. It is no longer solely through ritual and ceremony that one cultivates merit, but also through actions in one's practical daily life" (Chen 2002, 228–9). This orientation extends the relevant community beyond the limits of the ethnic and religious community. It also leads to inter-religious dialogue and co-operation.

CONCLUSION

It is not only individuals who are affected by the interaction with the mainstream society; the religious organizations of the minority are also transformed in some regards in the process of integration. First, members need assistance in coping with the day-to-day requirements of functioning in the new society, and they often turn to the religious organizations of their community for it. Second, their progressive integration into the mainstream tends to make them less and less interested in participating in the religious organizations of their own community. To meet this challenge, religious organizations take steps to prevent the loss of members and to avoid becoming gradually less relevant. Third, they need to address the "dissonance" between their own doctrines, moral prescriptions, rituals, and religious practices and the various features of their new social and cultural environment.

As a result, minority religious organizations become agents of acculturation and, in the process, gradually become integrated into the social matrix of the larger society. For instance, in order to remain relevant for community members and ensure their continued participation, religious organizations develop programs of various sorts to help their members with the problems they encounter in their new social and economic environment. Generally, integration is facilitated if there is a community to help with the social and moral problems encountered by the members.

Minority religious organizations may also offer a paradigm through which the new society is defined and interpreted. Specifically, the diffusion of the *embrace* and *selective engagement* paradigms would lead to the blurring of social boundaries between various groups in the society and, as a result, contribute to the acculturation and integration of newcomers.

6

The Transformation of Minority Religious Organizations

In his analysis of the life-cycle of ethnic churches, Mullins (1987, 1988, 1989) points out that over time, religious organization in ethnic communities have to satisfy different demands. The needs of the immigrant are usually different from those of the second and third generations. In addition, with acculturation and increasing participation in the larger society, the appeal of ethnic churches tends to gradually decrease. If the loss of relevance and the resulting weakening or even disappearance of the church is to be prevented, new organizational forms may be needed and new patterns of relationship and communication between the clergy and the laity may be required. Modifications in rituals and religious practices may also be necessary.

Generally, these transformations reveal a process of organizational integration into the mainstream society. The changes are introduced so as to draw the minority community into the religious matrix of the larger society and to enhance the church's status as a legitimate and equal addition to it. This process, for example, appears to have been the goal of Hmong refugees in Ontario when they adopted activities and pursuits modelled on those of the mainstream and Mennonite churches (Winland 1992, 111–12). The same kind of process was observed among Hindus in Trinidad: the adoption of "westernized, even Christian-like, forms may be interpreted as a drive to achieve greater 'respectability' in the eyes of the non-Hindu majority" (Vertovec

1990, 232). Some studies have found that the second generation, which often pursue higher education, are frustrated with "foreign" imams who are ignorant of local conditions and maintain "outdated" ideas and lifestyles (Naguib 2002, 169).

The patterns of transformations over time and especially over generations may be different for Christian and non-Christian religious institutions. As noted earlier, for earlier waves of immigrants, integration into the society did not involve abandoning the old religion in favour of another religious tradition, in large part because earlier immigrants belonged primarily to the same Judeo-Christian tradition as the members of the host society. But this distinction should not be overemphasized. First, there are a number of more or less different Christian churches and denominations in the mainstream society. Second, the Christianity of a number of immigrant communities had ritualistic and normative features different from those of the mainstream Christian churches.

When immigrants come to a society in which their own religion is not culturally and institutionally established, minority churches are confronted with particular organizational challenges. For example, Min (1992, 1391) points out that the religious challenges faced by Koreans is different from those faced by European-origin groups, "particularly because Protestantism is not a Korean national religion, such as Catholicism was for earlier Italian and Polish immigrants. In their effort to preserve the Korean subculture and identity through Christian churches, Korean immigrants have significantly 'Koreanized' Christianity."

At least four areas of transformation undertaken by religious organizations in response to the constantly changing situations in which they find themselves are dealt with in the research literature: (1) changes in organizational structure and roles; (2) modification of the religious ideas, symbols, and practices; (3) attempts to be more inclusive and, as a result, multi-ethnic; and (4) changes in the importance that community members attach to religion reflected in a decline in church attendance. Such a change would tend to decrease the influence of religious leaders and may lead to a shift in the relative importance of religious and secular organizations in the community.

CHANGES IN ORGANIZATIONAL
STRUCTURE AND ROLES

A category of adaptive responses involves transformations in the structure and goals of religious organizations and in the definition of organizational roles.[1] For instance, it has been observed in some Muslim communities that the mosque has evolved from being simply a place to pray to a centre of social activity and learning. This evolution is seen as a reversion to the dynamic role of the mosque in the days of the Prophet. Thus, the organizational change is not perceived as a departure from the principles of the religion but rather as attempts to return to its roots (Yang and Ebaugh 2001, 278).

Some changes introduced are part of a process of organizational acculturation, of adapting church organizations to a new socio-cultural environment. Abu-Laban (1983, 87) identifies three problem areas that pose serious challenges to religious leaders in Islamic communities. First, there is the difficulty of reaching the new, Canadian-born generation. This includes the challenge for imams of combining their religious training with a knowledge of the North American way of life. The second challenge, which stems from the high degree of national and linguistic diversity within the Islamic population, is how to integrate them into a coherent whole. Third, there is the need to reconsider Islamic law in order to reconcile the Islamic faith with the new socio-cultural system.

The organizational transformations include changes in the role of the clergy and of the laity. It was observed several years ago by Herberg (1960) that the roles of ministers in different religions become more and more like one another in response to cultural influences from the larger society. McDonough and Hoodfar (2005, 139–40) point out that the *imam* concept has had somewhat different meanings in different social contexts. Its root meaning is to guide or lead, but there have been variations in the specific ways in which that has been applied.

Although the *guru* has always been a part of the traditional Hinduism in India, the *guru*'s rule has expanded (Coward and

Botting 1999). "For many, the guru now becomes the heart of Hinduism, or Hinduism personified, allowing Hindus in Canada to feel that they are still Hindu in spite of the fact that they no longer engage in the full traditional patterns" (Coward 2000, 163). This increase in the importance of the guru took place, in part, because the specialists required for a full-scale ritual life are not regularly available in most Canadian cities and towns.

The changes that may take place include a shift of responsibility for the governance of the church organizations from the clergy to the laity. This may occur somewhat spontaneously because immigrants build their congregations from scratch and, as a result, assume leadership and participatory roles that often do not exist for the laity in the country of origin. An expansion in the role of the laity may also be due to the difficulty of finding priests or ministers either in the local community or from the country of origin. But it could also be encouraged by the clergy themselves in order to strengthen the identification of lay members with the institution.

Canadian legal requirements may also be a factor in the shift from clergy to laity. In the country of origin, the clergy may administer their temples, but "in Canada each temple needs a board of directors in order to comply with Canadian law ... and the boards of certain (Buddhist) temples are composed solely of lay members" (Boisvert 2005, 78).

Acculturation is also evident in the adoption of the congregational form in organizational structure and ritual. This is a form that is modelled on the American Protestant congregations and is usually unlike the religious institutions in the countries of origin. Congregationalism, which focuses on the local community as a congregation, includes, among its main features, increased voluntary participation of members in religious functions, a lay-centred community with lay leadership, and an expansion of services (Yang and Ebaugh 2001, 270–7). The adoption of westernized, even Christian-like forms by a non-Christian minority may be interpreted as a desire to achieve greater respectability in the eyes of the majority (Vertovec 1990, 229–32).

However, as Smith (1971, 242) emphasizes, even though some of the adaptive transformations are part of the process of acculturation, sometimes they have built on organizational changes that began in the cities of the homeland: "Tendencies toward voluntarism, lay initiative, and denominational pluralism in religion seem to have grown steadily in all urban societies during the last century, not only on both sides of the North Atlantic but on opposite shores of the South Atlantic, the Pacific, and the Indian Oceans."

Aside from their strictly religious roles, churches and religious leaders have engaged in various forms of community building. This has often taken place from the early phase of transplantation into a new environment (Jedwab 2001). Some of the organizational initiatives include the establishment of community centres and voluntary organizations that provide services to meet the needs of different segments of the membership, including the different generations (Bankston and Zhou 1996). Such organizations can be a source of individual and group empowerment. They provide opportunities for organized action in the pursuit of objectives derived from the group's particular needs. But perhaps "the special potency of religious institutions comes from the answers they give to a group's need for faith in the justice of their cause" (Warner 1993, 1069).

As a result, the religious or religiously controlled network of organizations becomes quite extensive. It tends to dominate community life and projects. It also provides the most opportunities for making gains in status, power, and influence and building social networks in the community (Min 1992, 1371). This opportunity structure is especially important if the members are deprived of power and status in the larger society. They can then aspire to achieve leadership in their own communal hierarchy (Min 1992, 1371–4; Mullins 1987; 1988).

Sometimes there are attempts to form regional, national, and international organizational networks, some comprising new denominations, others more loosely structured around limited common interests. If successful, such networks may increase the relevance of the religion and thus facilitate the retention of members or the recruitment of new members (Yang and Ebaugh 2001, 272–7).

Such organizations may be especially important for Muslim women. They can participate in different aspects of mosque life in ways that are not available to them in their homeland. This, of course, is much more the case in the second- and third- generation (Haddad 1983, 72). Perhaps more important is the significance of this involvement for the potential roles of women in public life in general: "Using religion to develop extra-domestic roles, [women] created powerful local and nation-wide single-sex organizations expressive of women's particular angers, anxieties, and demands" (Smith-Rosenberg, quoted by Warner 1993, 1072).

However, there can be obstacles to organizational adaptations such as the appointment of imams financed from outside. And a deterrent to acculturation may be the bureaucratization under umbrella organizations of Islamic institutions (Haddad 1983, 73). Wahhabism, a "puritanical and anti-mystical" variant of Islam that is promoted by Saudi Arabia by, for example, funding the building of mosques, may have a morally conservative and politicizing influence in certain mosques in Canada (McDonough and Hoodfar 2005, 141.

There can also be an opposite process in the religious community itself. For instance, it seems that at the beginning of the 1970s, a "reform" movement emerged with the aim of "purging Islam of innovations accumulated over the years and to eradicate unnecessary and un-Islamic patterns of acculturation." Although this movement has been strengthened by the arrival of new immigrants, it appears to be having only limited success, judging by the low rate of participation by mosques – between 1 and 5 per cent in the United States (Haddad 1983, 74–5).

MODIFICATION OF RELIGIOUS IDEAS, SYMBOLS, AND PRACTICES

Religion is embodied in doctrines, symbols, rituals, and various practices. Creative modifications take place not only in the organizational structures and roles but also in their doctrines, moral codes, symbols, and practices. Such transformations are part of the process of integration into the new society. Not only is the cultural environment different, but it is plural in terms of religion, attitudes towards religion (for example, expression in private prayers or in church attendance), moral values, and lifestyle. This challenge is probably more serious for non-Christian religious groups that come into a Christian cultural environment and for those coming from a largely homogeneous context. Attempts may be made "to achieve a symbiosis of a fundamentalist interpretation of Islam and the requirements of life in a modern, secular society" (Doomernik 1995, 53).

As noted above, leaders face the need to reinterpret Islamic beliefs and norms in order to reconcile their faith with the new socio-cultural system (Abu-Laban 1983, 87). The re-construction of the church in its identity and world view and the application of its basic principles in a different milieu are an ongoing process of accommodation to the new cultural environment – whether we call it inculturation, contextualization, or indigenization (Warner and Wittner 1998, 8). This process may be set in motion by members of the immigrant generation, but it will acquire momentum with the second and third generations.

Practices and rituals may also need to be transformed. Foremost among those is the adoption of the mainstream language as the language of religious services (Coward and Botting 1999, 45–6), which can be a contentious issue in the community (Chafetz and Ebaugh 2002). Also, in some cases, worship practices, such as the use of pews to replace floor sitting are borrowed from Christianity. In lieu of the traditional cycles of worship and sacred holidays, those embedded in the surrounding Christian culture may be adopted. (For example, the major worship ceremonies may be moved to Sundays.) One author has suggested "that having a ceremony on Sunday is a strategy used to appear more North American, more Christian, and therefore, to facilitate integration" (Rutledge 1991, 182). But there are also very practical reasons for weekend services, given the way economic and social activities are patterned in Western societies (Boisvert 2005, 75–8).

Thus, religious ideas, texts, rituals, symbols, and institutions are redeployed in a uniquely Canadian way. To conform to Canadian customs, a greater flexibility with regard to religious prescriptions (such as those pertaining to prayers five times a day) may become acceptable. As Bramadat (2005, 13–14) points out, "this re-creation happens neither *in toto* nor *ex nihilo* – rather, newcomers remake Islam, Buddhism, Hinduism, etc., in Canada out of a combination of old and new building resources."

Adaptations to the cultural environment may be reflected in the architecture of mosques or temples. In Muslim communities, such attempts pertain mostly to the issue of gender. To what extent are women to be welcome in the mosque? Are they to be segregated during prayer? Should they have a separate entrance? Such adaptations usually generate considerable debate in the community between "reformists" and traditionalists. However, it is significant that the issues are addressed at all and that in a number of cases, modifications are eventually adopted. A facilitating factor is the existence of diversity – ethnic and religious – among Muslims in Canada and, of course, the fact that decisions on such matters are not made by the state (Mossman 2011).

Among Hindus in Canada, funeral rituals associated with funerals have been adapted to Canadian practices. This includes the gathering around the body at a funeral home that consists in a welcome and eulogy, a ritual conducted by the priest, an invocation of Lord Vishnu, and a *mantra* from the Upanishads. The treatment of the body before cremation is also different than in India (Coward and Botting 1999, 42). In short, modifications are made "so as to accommodate funeral directors, the law, and the technology associated with cremation"(43).

These accommodations reveal the inventiveness of community members and leaders in the (re)interpretation of their traditional values and practices (Winland 1993, 112). The processes of ethnic- and religious-identity formation, continuity, and change are processes involving creative leadership and debate in the minority community. It is also the outcome of complex processes of negotiation among different groups in the community and in the larger society. Usually, such processes evolve over a fairly long time.

Even communities that seek to maintain a separation from the rest of society may have to undergo changes in the face of circumstances brought about by urbanization and modernization. Such changing circumstances have affected, for example, the Mennonite community. The geographic boundaries have become more and more urbanized and dispersed. Social networks, previously reinforced within the closed Mennonite communities, have been modified. Such phenomena have brought about a variety of responses, "ranging from the construction of social and geographical boundaries buttressing Mennonites from the encroachment of the wider society to an enthusiastic embracing of secular institutions and values." This has led to "the dismantling of norms concerning appropriate behaviour and role expectations for many as well as the creation of a vacuum in which competing interpretations and viewpoints on Mennonite identity have flourished" (Winland 1993, 116). Such an analysis is no doubt applicable, *mutatis mutandis*, to other groups in situations of social and cultural change.

At least two key processes have been identified as part of this adaptive transformation of the religious identity. First, leaders and members seek to emphasize the "universal" elements of their faith and adopt a "transnational" form of their religion (McDonough and Hoodfar 2005, 134). For example, since their initial introduction to the new environment, Hindus have been both inadvertently and intentionally modifying their beliefs and practices towards a unitary Hinduism in which beliefs and practices that were associated with a local or caste-based tradition in India are abandoned in favour of a homogenized, essentially Brahmanic tradition.

A second related process is "pristinization," that is, a return to the theological foundations of the religion. Reaching toward theological foundations is part of the attempt to separate religion from culture, a process discussed earlier. It is also part of the search for the "universal" since the theological foundation must be common to all members, whatever their national or ethnic backgrounds (Chafetz and Ebaugh 2002, x; Yang and Ebaugh 2001, 278–81). Pristinization is part of the accommodation to the new environment. However, it also occurs because of the need to justify and legitimate many of the changes in rituals and organization undertaken in the process of organizational acculturation. This may entail distinctions between what is fundamental and what is less so. In Islam, the fundamentals include the belief in one God, the existence of the prophet Mohammed, and salvation (for Shi'ites, there are five fundamentals). In addition, there are five pillars: the profession of faith, praying five times a day, almsgiving, annual fasting, and a pilgrimage to Mecca for all those able to make the journey. Muslims will still be considered Muslim if they do *not* practise the five pillars, but not if they disagree with any of the three basic principles (Sutton and Vertigans 2005, 20–1; Yousif 1993, chap. 1).

ATTEMPTS TO BE MORE INCLUSIVE

A third response to the new environment consists in attempts by congregations to become more inclusive in their membership so as to ensure the "critical mass" needed in order to establish and operate a church, mosque, or temple (Chafetz and Ebaugh 2002). Accordingly, attempts may be made to reach beyond the traditional boundaries to include people of different ethnic and national backgrounds (Yang and Ebaugh 2001, 281–3). This may also occur "spontaneously" through mixed marriages or deliberately through the search for converts.[2]

Boisvert (2005, 75) notes that there have been endeavours to bring together the various Buddhists communities in the celebration of Veshaka, the anniversary of the birth, enlightenment and death of Siddartha, which is an important event for Buddhists. Such a co-religious activity can be seem "as an opportunity to create a more universalistic mode of Buddhist belief and practice (since it cuts) across the various ethnic, national, linguistic, and particularistic modes of religious expression" (McLellan 1999, 31). As a result, the religious organizations are not only more likely to survive, but, significantly, they may also become multi-ethnic, much like mainstream churches of the larger society (Mullins 1987, 327).

An inclusive orientation may spring from the religious approach favoured by different churches. This is illustrated by the study of the Catholic and Evangelical Salvadoran communities mentioned above. The "communitarian ethic" of one led its leaders and members to reach out to and unite a large and ethnically diverse membership. The focus on individual salvation of the other oriented efforts to bring conversion to its smaller and more ethnically homogeneous membership (Menjivar 2003).

It is possible that the relationship works both ways: a particular religious orientation may lead to ethnic homogeneity or heterogeneity, but the fact that a congregation is characterized by one or the other may influence its religious orientation. The Salvadoran study referred to above suggests the first pattern. The latter is suggested by a comparison of two Korean-American churches with a different ethnic composition. Both promote the idea of the responsibility to care for people outside their own ethnic group, but their understanding of such responsibilities is different. In the ethnically homogeneous church, "implicitly Korean Americans adopt a spiritual version of the American Dream and connect Christianity to working hard and not complaining about discrimination, poverty, or other life problems" (Ecklund 2005, 21). "Because they emphasize class rather than ethnic or racial identities they have few narrative resources to create bridges with the non-white, non-Korean, impoverished residents" (23). In contrast, in the multi-ethnic church, "a religiously motivated commitment to ethnic diversity is promoted as part of its model of civic responsibility ... a responsibility to help those who are different from them."

The evolution towards "symbolic ethnicity and religiosity" may be a factor in the breaking down of ethnic and religious boundaries among members of a particular religion. The hypothesis would be that, with the erosion of cultural and religious particularities of the various religious subgroups in the larger religious collectivity, a sense of community could emerge across the variety of national, ethnic, social and cultural backgrounds of the adherents to the religion (Naguib 2002, 166).

SHIFTS IN THE RELATIVE IMPORTANCE OF RELIGIOUS AND SECULAR ORGANIZATIONS

As a result of their adaptation to the new environment and to the changing needs of their membership, religious organizations may become more focused on the strictly religious, leaving other functions to secular organizations in the community. In other words, they may become more specialized. Such a shift implies that secular organizations are formed in the community, sometimes at the instigation and with the support of the churches themselves and sometimes in competition with them.

As noted above, Gans (1994, 58) has suggested that religious groups tend to be "dominated by formally organized denominations in which informal groups play interstitial roles." In contrast, associations and informal groups tend to characterize the organization of ethnic groups. To the extent that this is the case, the hypothesis would be that, over time, religious organizations would predominate over secular organizations in ethnic communities.

However, in addition to associations and informal groups, the community may include formal organizations that are not religious, such as commercial, recreational, and media organizations. The relative importance of religious and secular organizations has to do with their respective capacity to absorb their members' lives, to structure their social relations, and motivate their participation in its social life and organizational activities. In other words, one of the important questions in this connection is whether the members of the community are more likely to become integrated into its religious or its secular organizational system.

The capacity to absorb the members' lives is partly defined by its potential for socialization, for orienting and regulating behaviour through rewards and sanctions, and for generating loyalty, attachment, and a sense of obligation to a particular group. Some forces favour the formation and vitality of religious organizations, and some favour secular organizations. Of course, the relative strength of these forces can vary enormously from one community to another or among different segments of its members.

The symbolic potential of the collectivity depends, in part, on the capacity of its cultural elite to re-construct a community as a meaningful cultural-symbolic reality in the new environment. Cultural entrepreneurs, however, need symbolic resources for such an undertaking. The symbolic construction of a community is intimately connected with the actual experience of the collectivity *qua* collectivity. There can be no significant symbolic construction without some elements of collective experience. The community or society as a cultural entity has both the potential and limitations of its distant and contemporary experience. Cultural resources cannot be created out of nothing. Cultural entrepreneurs[3] need symbolic resources in order to construct or reconstruct the collectivity as a cultural entity. There must be some sort of collective experience on the basis of which a definition of membership – a history, a societal role, and a view of the future – can be shaped. The emergence and achievements of cultural entrepreneurs are probably much more a function of the richness of the collective experience than of their own characteristics as individuals.

Ethnic and cultural collectivities vary considerably in how eventful their collective experience has been (Breton 1992). The nature of the experience can also vary. It can, for example, be primarily negative (marked, for example, by persecution, discrimination, military defeats, poverty, internal conflicts, and factional disputes) or primarily positive (consisting, for example, of economic, scientific, and cultural achievements; success in overcoming discrimination and disasters; an effective social and political organization; and institutions with distinctive characteristics). With subsequent generations, ethnic groups and organizations have a smaller and smaller cultural repertoire than religious groups on which to draw to sustain an active and dynamic community life.

A possible hypothesis is that the potential for symbolic innovation is greater among religious than secular leaders. By their very nature, religious institutions have more symbolic resources at their disposal than secular organizations and associations. These resources are identity-related, moral, and social. They can be used to define the identity of members, orient their behaviour, and define their moral and social obligations. And with an organizational structure and links to other communities across ethnic groups and countries, religious groups may have a greater cultural repertoire to sustain a community experience as opposed to purely private and family experiences. Religions also have a doctrinal heritage and frequently a class of people devoted to exploring it and making it relevant in different contexts. As a result, it seems that churches may have greater potential for attracting membership than ethnic groups (Gans 1994, 579).

"The plausibility of a group's belief depends on the strength of a supporting structure of social support. Group resources that support belief include affirmative therapies that are designed to still doubts and lapses of beliefs, rituals that reiterate beliefs, and ideological legitimations that confirm beliefs" (Billings 1990, 9–10). Thus, to the extent that these "supporting structures of support" are more religiously than non-religiously based, religious attachments and identities rather than ethic attachments will tend to prevail.

In addition, it may make a difference if the religion of the minority is different from that of the mainstream society. On the one hand, if the minority and mainstream religious institutions are of the same religious tradition, the minority institutions are not likely to be able to compete with those of the mainstream for members, at least not over generations. This is also the case of the non-religious institutions. On the other hand, if the religious tradition of the minority is different, its religious institutions may enjoy a sort of monopoly over its members and be able to retain their adherence and obtain conformity to its practices. There would then be greater integration into the religious minority community and, correspondingly, less acculturation into the mainstream religious tradition.

However, the collective historical experience of the community may not be related to its religion. It may be related to its language, its attempts at economic survival and development (such as by the formation of co-operatives), historical events in the country of origin or in the society of adoption, the role played by the minority community in the settlement of a region of the country, experiences of systematic discrimination, and so on. That is not to imply that religious organizations were not involved in these events and collective experiences, but that those events and experiences were not religious. They are part of the community's ethno-cultural, not religious history.

In many cases, leaders of religious organizations played a critical role in community building and development, at least in the early phase of settlement in a new environment. Because of this, the religious domain tended to be the main arena in which the competition for status took place. The social and political dynamics of the community tended to occur in that domain. However, with time, secular organizations, such as community centres, cultural and political organizations, and trade associations, were established. This sometimes led to tensions between clerical leaders, who had up to then controlled the institutional system of the community, and lay leaders, who not only sought more influence in the religiously controlled organizations, but who attempted to establish domains in which they would be dominant.

In her study of the Polish-American community, Znaniecki-Lopata (1976, 50) mentions a "long, strong, and eventful competition between leaders attempting to organize [the community] under the banner of religion, and those focusing on nationalism and other themes." The latter were the winners of the prolonged conflict although, as time went by, the two sides reached a compromise for the sake of community maintenance and vitality.[4] As a result of such competitive struggles, at least some control of community organizations and services tends eventually to shift to secular groups in ethnic communities as it did in mainstream society, where the state took over many of the services traditionally provided by churches. The policy of multiculturalism, with its underlying philosophy that concedes some measure of autonomy (and legitimacy) to community leaders to govern their communities and with the symbolic and material support it provided, no doubt contributes to the shift in the composition of the leadership (Jedwab 2001; Macey 1999, 861).

Moreover, if the religious inter-organizational system has more access to symbolic resources, the non-religious may have greater access to instrumental resources for integrating members of the community. This is especially so if its leaders of the non-religious organizational system are able to link it to organizations of the larger society. The system may include such organizations as businesses, mutual aid societies, agencies for the integration of newcomers, insurance agencies, political groups that manage affairs within the community and in relations to mainstream institutions, and educational and cultural centres.

Finally, external circumstances may also have a significant influence on the relative power and status of different institutional areas in the community. For instance, in an officially secular state, government agencies and political parties tend to prefer to deal with secular rather than religious organizations. To the extent that this is so, it would encourage the formation and maintenance of non-religious ethnic or cultural community organizations and provide arenas for gains in leadership and social status in those areas.

CONCLUSION

The process of integration entails modifications in religious organizations, such as changes in liturgical practices, leadership roles, and various aspects of organizational functioning. These are responses to the new cultural environment and to the constantly changing circumstances in which minorities find themselves. Three areas of transformation have been explored by researchers: (1) changes in organizational structure and roles; (2) reinterpretation or adaptation of traditional doctrines, normative prescriptions, and liturgical practices in such a way that they make sense in the new social and cultural environment; (3) attempts to be more inclusive with the result that they become multi-ethnic. The reinterpretations and adaptations made, as well as the social processes though which they are "negotiated," would be fruitful areas of research.

There may also be a shift in the relative importance of religious and secular organizations as a result of the evolution of religious commitments and practices of community members and a related decline in the influence of religious leaders in the community. Research is needed on the extent and patterns of competition between religious and secular organizations (and their leaders) for power and influence in the community and as representatives of the community in relations with mainstream organizations, such as government agencies, community organizations, and the media.

PART FOUR

Minority Religions in Relation to the Larger Society and Its Institutions

It was seen in previous chapters that minority religious groups adapt their institutions and practices to fit into the mainstream society. But the adaptation to the new cultural environment could also consist in seeking public affirmation of the "new" religion and attempting to obtain recognition of it by the institutions (for example, political, cultural, educational) of the larger society. These two modes of integration – adaptation and demands for recognition – are not incompatible. Adapting to a new environment does not necessarily imply a loss of distinctive identity.

The recognition of the "new" religions and their incorporation into the institutional matrix of the society are important elements in the integration of newcomers. Of course, one dimension of the integration of minorities has to do with individual social, economic, and political rights, and equality of treatment in social and institutional settings. But the integration of minorities entails more than the integration of individuals; it also entails the recognition of new religious communities, that is, the institutional incorporation of the religion itself into the cultural and institutional fabric of the larger society (Koenig 2005a, 2009; Kastoryano 2004, 1235). In other words, integration involves cultural-group rights such as the recognition of religious communities, as well as individual rights (Minkenberg 2008).*

---

* This distinction seems to be included in the one between the right to equality and the right to difference (Taylor 1992; Schiffauer 2007).

These two dimensions of integration – individual and collective – can be mutually reinforcing. Indeed, the recognition of
minority non-Christian religions by societal institutions – state,
educational, media, and established churches – can have a positive influence on the integration of individuals. The dynamics
involved in the search for recognition concerns the social status
of the minority religion in the larger society and its acceptance
as a legitimate part of the society. Individuals seek a positive
self-image. One's self-image is shaped partly by the social es-
teem received from others as a result of one's own behaviour.
However, it is also related to the status that one's community
and its institutions are awarded in the society, to the acknow-
ledgment of their social and cultural worth (Bastenier 1998;
Taylor 1992). In this way, the recognition of a minority and
its religious (and other) institutions is a significant part of
social integration.

It is hypothesized that if minority religious *institutions* became progressively "Canadianized," that is, if they became part
of the mainstream set of religious institutions, their members
would be integrated into the society more easily. Reciprocally,
the social, economic, and cultural integration of individuals
could facilitate the incorporation of their religious institutions.

A critical issue, then, has to do with the modalities of institutional incorporation of the minority religious communities
and institutions. Two important questions will be examined
in this connection. First, to what extent is there pressure from
minority religious groups on the larger society either to re-
shape its institutions so as to grant some form of recognition
to the minority religious groups or to extend to the newly
emerging communities the support and services provided by
public institutions (Kastoryano 2004, 1235–6)? Second, what
features of the mainstream institutional and cultural climate
prevailing in mainstream society can affect the possibilities
for mutually acceptable arrangements?

The Pursuit of Recognition
by the Larger Society

The building of churches, mosques, temples, or other manifestations of their religion in the public sphere is part of the process by which newcomers make the new society their own; once these are established, a certain degree of cultural acculturation by the institution itself would tend to follow its recognition and acceptance. This hypothesis has been stated by Smith (1971, 243). He argued that "what these new citizens demanded in their religious life, once they determined to stay here, was the right to do what their predecessors of the three major faiths had done – to fashion religious communities suited to their own needs ... None should be surprised that once the right was granted or gained, the congregational and denominational organizations they founded resembled those which earlier settlers had established."

Institutional recognition is part of what religious newcomers expect. Members of a community whose institutions and culture are defined as "alien," as intruders who don't fit in "our" culture will tend to be resentful, to feel alienated, and to remain at the margins of the society. The wish to build mosques or temples symbolizes the desire to cease to be considered alien and become rooted in society (Sander 1991, 71). It is also a demand for the right to be different. Thus, the recognition by public authorities and the public of the newcomers' community and its institutions – and its differences – as an established feature of the society would, in all likelihood, convey the message that they belong, and that, in turn, would facilitate their integration into the larger society (Kastoryano 2004, 1237–8).

Alba (2005, 30) discusses the process of "institutional incorporation" in the case of Jews in the United States. He notes that "over time, the formerly immigrant religions have become part of the American mainstream ... [and] the religions as practiced have certainly changed during the course of this incorporation into the mainstream: for instance, non-Orthodox forms of Judaism, including Reform Judaism, with its muted religious services and commitments, found wide acceptance in the United States and what had been a minor holiday in the Jewish calendar, Hanukah, was elevated in status to provide Jewish children with their equivalent to Christmas." This appears to have been an instance of institutional integration leading to the integration of individuals.

Kurien (1998, 37) points out that "becoming Hindu" and "becoming American" may not be mutually exclusive if Indian immigrants establish a Hindu-American community and identity, as would be much easier if Hinduism became part of the religious institutional matrix of the society. The pressure that minority religious groups exert on societal institutions for some form of incorporation into the institutional matrix frequently triggers social and political controversies and processes. Three sets of issues are considered in this connection: (1) the types of claims made by religious minorities and their articulation; (2) the extent of support from members of the religious minority; and (3) patterns of controversies and their resolution.

TYPES OF CLAIMS AND THEIR ARTICULATION

As noted above, the search for recognition goes beyond the adaptation of the minority religious organizations to the new cultural context. Religious leaders may formulate various types of claims for recognition and accommodation, claims that could be taken to express a desire to become integrated into the society. Among the different claims made, the most frequent are those seeking acceptance and respect for the community's symbols and practices, such as religious holidays, dress, and objects like the *kirpan*.

Establishing burial grounds can also be a very important part of the "settlement" of the community because it involves an element of necessity. "A Jewish community does not need a synagogue to practice the faith but, "in order to properly bury its dead, a consecrated cemetery is a must ... The existence of a cemetery and the associated burial rituals "is a mark that the culture has found a new home" (Laidlaw 2008). "The symbolic bond that ties roots to soil, land, and geography is expressed clearly in times of death. Finding consecrated ground in which to bury one's dead is, in my opinion, one of the most eloquent signs of settlement and integration" (Naguib 2002, 168).

Another type of claim concerns places of worship (such as temples, mosques, and synagogues) and has to do mostly with access to space for the erection of buildings but also, more broadly, for the explicit identification of sacred space (as in the case of *eruv* in Orthodox Jewish communities).[1] Closely related is the establishment of schools that are recognized and even subsidized by the state.

Finally, there is the claim for the recognition of community organizations and their leaders as representative of the community – a recognition that would result in consultations and negotiations with them on matters of interest to the religious minority.

The articulation of claims, however, is a political process that requires organization, leadership, the mobilization of resources and social support, and the formation of social networks (Koenig 2009, 306). And since the institutional structures of the country of origin cannot be simply duplicated in the host countries, members of minority religions have to create new organizations and structures of authority appropriate to their new environment (Cesari 2004b, 124). This usually involves competition. That is to say, "internal leadership has to be earned; very few leaders, collective or individual, can move into an ascribed position" (Nielsen 1991, 54). This may be an obstacle to the articulation of claims on behalf of the community.

Another possible obstacle stems from characteristics of the members of the religious collectivities themselves. Foremost among those is the internal diversity along lines of national origin, ethnicity, race, and political orientation. Frequently, at least in the early phase, recruitment tends to be on an ethnic or national basis and even on narrower bases such as the clan, caste, region, or craft (Nielsen 1991, 55). Within the same religion, there can also be a variety of different traditions.

As in other large communities, the differentiation within minority religious groups tends to be accompanied by social, ideological, and economic cleavages (Doomernik 1995, 48; Roy 1992, 76; Khosrokhavar 1997, 261; Zolberg and Woon 1999, 5–6). From such differences frequently emerge divergent views and priorities about the collective goals to be pursued and the social and political strategies to be used for the development of the community and its integration in the larger society.

In addition, some degree of coherent institutionalization for the governance of the community needs to take place if it is to be recognized by mainstream institutions whether at the local, regional or national levels. Unless bridges are built across such divisions, institutional recognition by the larger society may be difficult, if not impossible. But internal differences and contextual factors often bring about competition among the community organizations, including mosques or temples, and their leaders. There may be several organizations attempting to mobilize the limited resources available within the community or from sources in the country of origin in order to establish their organizations and secure their leadership in the neighbourhood, city, region, or the country as a whole.

However, deliberate attempts to build some forms of unified organization may take place. For example, the use of the same temple by different ethnic and religious Hindu groups has helped draw Hindus together so that Hinduism has an organizational basis upon which to be recognized as a formal religion in Canada (Coward 2000, 155–6). In 1983, a national conference was organized to develop the constitution of the Hindu Council of Canada. Such processes have taken place in other groups as well (Banerjee and Coward 2005, 35). Another important factor in the progressive bridge-building process is the gradual assumption of the key positions in these organizations by members of the next generation, who do not necessarily have the same interests as their parents (Doomernik 1995, 52).

Features of the institutional conventions of the mainstream society may also be relevant. For instance, in Britain the legal criteria for setting up an organization are minimal. No registration is required, although there are tax advantages in satisfying the requirements of the Charity Commissioners. In contrast, in Belgium and France, organizations are required to have a minimum number of Belgian or French citizens in their leadership. This has been an obstacle to the formation of organizations that are able to negotiate with public authorities. Indeed, the elimination of this requirement in 1981 in France led to an increase in the number of organizations (Nielsen 1991, 48).[2]

Opposition from groups or institutional leaders in the larger society may also foster unity in the minority community. "In France, mobilizations around the head scarf issue have strengthened the leadership of Islamic associations as representatives of a community taking shape around Islam. The French state, by selecting imams as interlocutors in order to calm tensions, has inadvertently increased the negotiating power of the religious associations by excluding others or forcing them into the Islamic sphere" (Kastoryano 2004, 1240).

Chen (2002, 231–3) presents a paradoxical case in this regard. Because of the similarity of the evangelical Grace Taiwanese Church to mainstream evangelical churches, it does not have the burden of engaging in public-relations work. This similarity, however, prevents it from being seen as an adequate representative of the Chinese community by representatives of mainstream organizations or politicians. The Chinese Buddhists are less well accepted because they are different, but they are seen as better representatives of multiculturalism.

SUPPORT FOR THE PUBLIC EXPRESSIONS OF RELIGION

Is there among minority religious groups support for the public expression and institutionalized recognition of their religion? A secondary question is whether the support is found primarily among immigrants and whether there is a significant decline in the second generation. This question is highly relevant since large proportions of members of the minority religious groups are immigrants.

According to Khosrokhavar (1997, 263) many middle-class Muslims in France who are socially and economically integrated feel they may have much to lose from public manifestations of their religion. They prefer to express their religiosity in private. According to the author, this is the official position of some mosques and associations that seek to ease their acceptance in the society and, accordingly, consider it better to compromise on certain practices and avoid public displays of their religion. To what extent this is so in Canada and the United States needs to be investigated.

In addition, to the extent that the level of religious practice, the degree of theological knowledge, and the importance attached to the religion are moderate or weak among adherents of minority religions – as seems to be somewhat the case (Roy 1992, 79–80) among, for example, young Muslims in France – support by the religious minority for institutional recognition by the larger society can be expected to be fairly weak.

Another type of obstacle to the articulation of claims for institutional recognition is the theological orientation and institutional strategies of a church. Some research discussed earlier[3] found that a focus on individual salvation and a mission of personal evangelism tends to restrict members to their own congregation, which tends to be of their own ethnic group. In contrast, a "communitarian ethnic" that focuses on charity and good works tends to be associated with an outreach strategy that goes beyond one's own group, religious or ethnic. One is oriented to the group itself while the other sees its mission in terms of a contribution to society.

In this context, it is worthwhile considering the different ways (identified by Bader 2009) in which minority groups are regulated. There is, first, the distinction between internal and external regulation. That is, there are processes of governance in religious communities concerned with the identification of patterns of integration and the types of claims made to societal institutions that would be acceptable to most members of the minority community. There are also two categories of external regulation: governmental and non-governmental. The first category is discussed in the next chapter. The second refers to "more voluntary and democratic forms of self-regulation by interfaith networks, movements, associations, and ecumenical organizations" (Bader 2009, 46). The influence of such inter-organizational environments and networks needs to be examined empirically.

The reluctance by certain members of minority religions to seek recognition may be partly due to their perception of negative attitudes in the larger society.[4] Such attitudes can be experienced by members of minority religions in their attempts to find places to hold religious services. Some of these attitudes are simply based on negative stereotypes, but some are based on conceptions of what the character of public institutions should be in the society – specifically conceptions pertaining to the separation of church and state. Whatever their content, negative stereotypes and attitudes indicate a lack of receptivity that may act as a disincentive to the pursuit of recognition.

In addition, the desire to integrate into the society may also be an equally if not more powerful disincentive to seek institutional recognition of the minority religion. The idea that immigrants and their children do not seek integration and acculturation is not supported by empirical evidence in Canada and the United States, as shown in a review of the research literature (Reitz and Breton 1994). Although the research reviewed pertained primarily to European-origin groups, it is a safe hypothesis that similar results would be found among recent non-European immigrants. Of course, this needs to be investigated empirically.

That does not mean that social recognition of the religion is not desired. The fact that private rather than public religious practice is favoured among many immigrants does not mean that they do not want their religious to be considered both as legitimate and socially respectable, and an integral part of the religious institutional matrix of the society. Most immigrants, whatever their religious affiliation and level of practice, would be profoundly offended if their religion were rejected as out of date and not worth the attention of intelligent people – as many religions are in books, articles, and media reports. The search for acceptance as a legitimate institution is part of the search for status in the society, as pointed out above. However, the fact that some form of recognition is desired does not imply a willingness to make it an issue of public policy.

CONTROVERSIES AND THEIR RESOLUTION

Whenever a search for a public recognition takes place, it tends to generate tensions and confrontations between the minority religious groups and those in the mainstream community who resist such recognition or accommodation. As Leveau (1991, 131) points out, "the wish to compromise expressed by the majority of both groups as well as the steps ahead made by both sides ... must not let them forget that on each side a minority group (of 1/4 or 1/3) exists which, either through its demands or its refusal is capable of ruining any effort towards a synthesis" (Leveau 1991, 131). But, as will be seen, it seems that most such controversies are resolved through more or less informal negotiations and that it is at the local – rather than the regional or national – level that controversies are the most easily resolved.

There are differences of opinion in the mainstream population as to whether any formal recognition should be given to relatively new and growing religious communities. And among those who are inclined to grant recognition to new religions, there is debate about the institutional forms that any recognition should take. Controversies over such issues have taken place and sometimes have been quite intense as shown when the possible introduction of *sharia* as part of the legal apparatus became an issue of public policy or when the public funding of religious schools was included in the platform of a political party.[5]

Some incorporation into the institutional matrix of the society is in fact taking place without any public controversies. Indeed, many day-to-day accommodations are negotiated quite regularly without creating any significant conflicts. The requests from minorities appear to be dealt with on a case-by- case basis until a pattern is established. In most professional fields (for example, education and health), the prevailing philosophy is that the desirable approach is to take account of the specifics of each case. General principles can guide decisions and actions, but they need to be applied to the particularities of each case and their application usually involves informal negotiation.

That is one of the main conclusions of the Consultation Commission on Accommodation Practices Related to Cultural Differences in Quebec (Bouchard and Taylor 2008, 27–34). Although based, not on systematic statistical analysis, but on a number of case studies, the evidence obtained by the commission on practices in the areas of education and health and with regard to religious holidays in the workplace in both public institutions and the business sector indicates that harmonious accommodations are the rule rather than the exception. Problems and difficulties do occur, but it seems that acceptable solutions are eventually negotiated. It seems that pragmatism leads people to modify their ways of thinking and behaving as they encounter new circumstances. Of course, additional research is needed to understand better how "harmonizations" take place in different circumstances.

There may also be cases where the accommodation is not controversial but rather the result of the pursuit of perceived mutual benefits. That seems to have been the case in Prince George, British Columbia. It was reported that "for years, the city has watched Muslim doctors, professors and engineers reject offers to settle in Prince George because the city has no mosque ... The B.C. Muslim Association decided to act ... (and) civic leaders are hoping that the multi-million Islamic cultural and educational centre will be a beacon that draws highly skilled professionals to a city that badly needs to diversify its forestry-dominated economy" (Armstrong 2009). There may be other cases of co-operation in the pursuit of mutually compatible interests. Again, research is needed.

But public controversies do occur in various communities. The research literature includes case studies of a number of negotiated arrangements that followed initial opposition and misunderstanding.

In a survey carried out in 1997, of the senior administrative staff of thirty-five municipalities asking whether there had ever been conflicts between minority groups and their municipal governments, seventeen responded that they had experienced at least one such dispute. In fourteen of those cases, the conflicts involved zoning disputes over land use. In nine, conflicts occurred over attempts to establish or enlarge mosques; in five, the conflict involved the character of Chinese retail malls or the location of funeral homes, and in two, it was over the location of a Jamaican community centre (Isin and Siemiatycki 2002, 196, 198).

In another survey in 1998, this time of full-service mosques, eight of the twenty-four (out of twenty-six) that responded to the survey indicated they encountered difficulties with location and zoning approval. Only three cases were particularly contentious and were not resolved at the local level but by a provincially appointed body – the Ontario Municipal Board. In all three cases, the conflict was resolved in favour of the mosques. And even in the contentions cases, the Islamic group received support from some members of the mainstream community, from newspaper editorials, and from Jewish and Catholic leaders (Isin and Siemiatycki 2002, 188).

In a study of *eruvim*[6] in Jewish Orthodox communities, it was found that in many cases, the *eruv* is established without controversy. This is partly because "there is no unreal quality to an *eruv* ... since it is impossible to know whether one is in an *eruv* or where its borders lie" (Siemiatycki 2005, 260).[7] Even in the same socio-political environment, one *eruv* may be controversial while another may not be. In Outremont, which is part of the City of Montreal, the issue emerged "in the late 1990s when members of the Hassidic community approached the municipality for approval to erect an *eruv*. There was no novelty in the request since the city of Montreal and four other smaller area municipalities already had *eruvim*. But in Outremont, an acrimonious debate took place (Siemiatycki 2005, 266).

In the conflicts where representatives of the religious minority, public authorities, and residents confront one another, a number of patterns can be observed. The public authorities experience the requests for the use of public space by a religious community as a challenge to the ways in which the school boards, city government, and municipal agencies conduct their business (James 2006, 51). For the minority, the challenge is to define the proper modes of acculturation to a changing demographic and cultural environment.

There is also an economic issue where places of worship are tax-exempt. As a result, the establishment of new churches, temples, or mosques can represent a loss of revenue, especially at times when the municipality sees the possibility of attracting new enterprises to the locality (Germain 2004, 433). There are corresponding issues for the residents, such as concerns with the possible decrease in the value of their property and the usual problems that emerge with any development such as traffic, parking, and noise.

Although the public debate may be articulated in terms of such pragmatic issues – which can, of course, be legitimate – the underlying issues may be social and cultural (Isin and Siemiatycki 2002). This basic issue is naturally defined differently by the established residents and by the newcomers. For the former, the arrival of the new religious minority may be perceived as a threat to the character of the neighbourhood as defined by its ethnic and religious composition. A minority seeking to express publicly its identity and culture may be considered a threat to their own identity, culture, and lifestyle. Considering the opposition to the establishment of an *eruv* in the community, Germain (2004, 440 – my translation) notes that "far from bearing on the concrete conditions of the cohabitation, the controversies in Outremont are but a pretext for articulating conflicts based on a clash of values and lifestyles, each seeing in the other a threat to its own identity. In fact, this dynamic is, for a good part, driven by a situation in which the francophone middle class (including European-origin immigrants) feels that it is being minoritized by a rapidly expanding Hasidic community ... This minority embodies all that

'French-Canadians' rejected with the Quiet Revolution: submission to the group, the submission of women, the ascendancy of religion in daily life, and its display in the public space."

For the religious minority, the issue is the acceptance of their difference and of establishing the same citizenship rights as those enjoyed by the mainstream community. This was, in fact, one of the arguments of the Ontario Municipal Board's adjudicator in his decision in favour of the establishment of a mosque. "He noted that all immigrants, dating back to Ontario's first European settlers, made a priority of establishing places of worship in their new land. The Anglicans had been privileged by the designation of Clergy Reserves – space specifically set aside for churches. Recent immigrants had to be more 'entrepreneurial and resourceful'" (Isin and Siemiatycki 2002, 200).

The process for dealing with the conflict may be informal or formal. Sometimes a body is established to deal with the matter. In the case of the Sikh *kirpan* in Peel region schools in Ontario, for example, a board of inquiry was set up by the Ontario Human Rights Commission. Representatives of the various groups and organizations concerned appeared before the board, which eventually decided in favour of those who wished to wear the *kirpan*, with some conditions (Wayland 1997, 547–9). In contrast, a study of religious pluralism in Kingston, Ontario, found that "generally, the adaptations have occurred through trial-and-error modifications, informal accommodations, ad hoc adjustments" (James 2006, 62).

There are cases, however, where the process can be characterized as a "judicial spiral" in which a succession of controversies eventually involves a higher judicial body. The debate, then, bears less and less on the concrete conditions of coexistences and more and more on matters of values, lifestyle, and cultural identity (Germain 2004, 438–40; Wayland 1997, 551–3).

BUILDING SOCIAL TRUST

Negotiations can be an opportunity for the building of trust between groups. But it seems that this is more likely to happen if the disagreements between groups are framed in practical terms so that negotiations are possible, or at least easier. In addition, a basic condition for the success of negotiations is a willingness to accept dialogue and compromise. Negotiations can thus be occasions for the building of trust. The existence of organizations or political parties that actively deny the legitimacy of particular minorities as social and political actors can make negotiations and the building of social trust very difficult. One of the central features of the discourse of right-wing political parties is the attempt "to delineate who 'the people' are and who does not and should not legitimately be part of the people – for example, groups representing racial and ethnic minorities who will not 'assimilate' into the desired culture" (Betz and Johnson 2004, 316; see also Rydgren 2007).

When the debate is framed around practical matters, compromises are reached with less conflict and acrimony than when it is cast in terms of identity or basic values. Indeed, "ideological negotiations" entail differences of principle which make compromises difficult. And, in contrast to practical matters, they are "hidden," a condition that can foster distrust.

Negotiations require communication among the interested parties: government authorities, representatives of the local community, and leaders of the minority religious communities (Cesari 2004a, 131). Both direct communication and communication through the media seem to be important. The first is the one through which practical arrangements are forged; the second is the one through which some consensus within the various communities can be reached. The character of the communications may influence considerably the level of social trust.

Organized interfaith contacts may also foster trust among communities. No systematic research was found on this important topic, but there are developments in this area. A significant innovation that could build social trust among religious groups is the new course introduced in Quebec public schools called Ethics and Religious Culture – which seeks to familiarize students with the religious diversity that exists in the world and in their own society.[8] It will, of course, take a few years before the influence of the course on attitudes and social relationships can be assessed empirically.

Occasionally, newspapers report activities that may increase social trust. Recently, fifty synagogues and mosques across North America were paired in an effort to expand interfaith dialogue. Members of each pair (Jewish and Muslim) join their counterparts for common activities, such as prayer, dinner, and discussions (Keung 2008). Another example is a report on sixteen congregations converging on three churches (Anglican, United, and Catholic) each Sunday, thus providing immigrants with occasions meet and "establish a community with others like themselves and learn to live in Canada" (Laidlaw 2007).

There is also informal evidence that the "selective engagement" paradigm discussed earlier (Mattson 2003) exists in some ethno-religious communities. This paradigm puts value on attempts to have a positive societal influence by adopting various social and political causes, such as environmentalism, social justice, and better access to education by the less advantaged in society. Such initiatives may result in social trust among groups. An illustration of such involvement is provided by the case of Muslim women[9] who reached beyond the mosque to help others by volunteering in election campaigns, taking part in environmental activities, and assisting disabled people (Gordon 2007). The hypothesis is that such involvement beyond the boundaries of one's group can build social trust.

Conversions could be a phenomenon resulting in a growth of trust between religious communities. However, almost no evidence could be found on the extent to which members of minority religions convert to the mainstream Christian religion and on the extent to which members of the mainstream religion convert to a minority religion. Would there be more social acceptance and institutional recognition of different religions if there were a "critical mass" of converts? Do converts increase the level of social trust and generate "bridging social capital" that would facilitate the incorporation of minority religions into the social matrix and reduce any threats to the cohesion of the society? It could be hypothesized that to the extent that conversions

bring about shared experiences and a feeling of common identity, they may reduce the social and cultural distance between
religious groups, increase trust, and facilitate co-operation
among their members.

Little empirical evidence seems to be available on such questions. However, some trends can perhaps be detected through an
analysis of patterns among people of multiple origins – a phenomenon on the rise in recent decades. A comparison of 1981
and 2001 census data shows that "given the rise in multiple ethnicity whatever the causes, the effect of multiple ethnicity is to
work against the increased religious pluralism of Canada because the consistent beneficiaries with few exceptions are Western
(Protestant and Roman Catholic) Christianity and the no religion category" (Beyer 2005, 191). In other words, there would
be a number of conversions to Christianity but few from
Christianity to minority religions. In Europe and in the United
States, however, a number of Christians seem to have converted
to Islam.

Several questions can be raised in this connection: what would
constitute a "critical mass" of conversions sufficient to affect the
quality of relations between religious groups? How does the history of relations between the religious groups impinge on the
possible influence of conversions? And in what circumstances
would conversions have either a positive or a negative impact on
inter-religious relations?

If they become fairly numerous, religious conversions – in
both directions, it should be emphasized – may raise questions in
the public consciousness about the defining features of the society's identity: "who is 'us' and who is the foreigner when people
are not of the same origin, when the relationship plays itself out
between natives and immigrants, but ones that share the same
religion, the same places of worship, and the same social networks of associations" (Allievi 1999, 284; my translation)?

A factor that may be beneficial to inter-religious relations is
the fact that some oriental religions, such as Buddhism, have
been adopted by New Age groups in Western countries. This may
facilitate the recognition of the minority religions in the larger

society – they become part of the search for meaningful spiritu-
alities and, accordingly, may be seen as being, to some extent,
part of the religious institutional fabric of the society (Obadia
2000, 68).

On the other hand, the effect of conversions could also be
negative, as when conversions are part of a movement of social
protest against a socio-economic and political order considered
to be unfair and discriminatory. This has been the case, to a certain extent, among groups of Blacks in the United States (Daynes
1999). In such circumstances, conversion to Islam would be seen
as a way to transform a racial stigma from a liability into an
asset. "Islam initially satisfied the desire for a distinct identity
within American society. More than just a spiritual movement,
Islam allowed African Americans, in the years following emanci-
pation, to address the question of their roots by creating a myth
of Black superiority and the Black race's original devotion to
Islam" (Cesari 2004a, 25).

However, from the perspective of the dominant group, the
adoption of Islam or another minority religion by subgroups
that express opposition to the existing economic and political
order may increase the sense that this religion is a social and
political threat. Thus, instead of increasing social trust, such conversions may reduce it. This is why it was pointed out that social
trust is more likely to be built when members of the mainstream
convert to minority religions. In their case, conversion would
tend to occur for very different reasons and, accordingly, have a
potentially positive rather than a negative effect on the building
of social bridges between groups.

CONCLUSION

Integration is a process that involves organizations as well as individuals. New or growing religious groups may seek to be recognized by the larger society and be integrated into its institutional
matrix. If the new religious groups are culturally different from
the mainstream, their cultural and institutional integration may
constitute an important challenge for the mainstream society.

A first question in this regard is to what extent religious minorities exert pressure for recognition and incorporation into the institutional matrix of the society. A related issue pertains to the conditions under which a sufficiently cohesive organizational structure emerges in the community so that claims for recognition can be articulated and negotiated.

A related matter is the attitudes of members of minority religions with regard to the extent and modes of recognition by institutions of the larger society. The variations in religious practice noted in an earlier chapter would suggest that there would be variations in attitudes about institutional recognition among adherents. However, little evidence seems to exist on this question. What proportion endorses the positions expressed by different community leaders? Are there variations by gender, social class, length of time in Canada, and generation in this regard? Generally, it seems that, although some communities or subgroups of communities attempt to exert pressure on public institutions for recognition, this does not seem to be a general pattern. The prevailing view in Western societies that religious practice is a private matter is progressively adopted by members of religious communities, particularly among second and subsequent generations.

There also appears to be a considerable range of views on the matter among adherents of established Judeo-Christian religions. Many Jews and Christians want some form of acceptance of their religion, even if it is only through the presence of churches or synagogues. But there are subgroups that want more, such as publicly funded schools or the right to wear religiously sanctioned dress or objects.

Research is clearly needed on this topic. Empirical evidence on the extent and social bases of support for various modes of recognition and accommodation would be useful, not only for a better understanding of the factors and processes of integration, but also of the processes of negotiations between representatives of minority religious groups and mainstream institutions.

8

The Incorporation of Minority Religions into Mainstream Institutions

Responses by institutional authorities to pressure from minority religious groups for some form of recognition depend to a considerable extent on the established institutional arrangements and practices and on the cultural climate prevailing in mainstream institutions. These include churches, media, schools, and the state but perhaps especially the latter since, in modern societies, state institutions tend to be central in social and economic governance. The different issues addressed in the research literature on this matter can be grouped under three broad questions: (1) what are some of the conditions for successful negotiations among concerned groups and organizations? (2) How do the institutional forms and culture in which they are embedded impinge on the extent and modes of incorporation? (3) What challenges do the particularities of the collective identity and of the national narrative represent for the recognition and incorporation of new minority religions?

SOME NEGOTIATION STRATEGIES

The case studies examined in the previous chapter showed that the response to controversial claims depends partly on the way in which the issues to be dealt with are defined. When the issue is defined as a matter of pragmatic arrangements, negotiations can result relatively easily in a successful compromise. But when the issues are defined as differences in culture and values, it is very difficult even to engage in negotiations. This is so because the compromises that are required when principles and identity-bound values are involved are difficult if not impossible. This was also observed in additional studies. For instance, in a comparison of the British and Swedish approaches to the matter of mosque building, it was observed that, in Britain, the discussion concerning the various issues seems to "revolve around whether a particular solution is practically possible and effective." In Sweden, on the other hand, the debate re-volves "around whether or not the underlying principles and the motives of Muslims are acceptable from a traditional Swedish point of view, or whether or not their motives are compatible with traditional Swedish manners and customs, norms, and values." The result is that Britain is more advanced in the institutionalization of Islam than Sweden, whether this involves matters such as the building of mosques and access to *halal* food in school or workplace cafeterias (Sander 1991, 80–1).

A similar contrast has been noted between the attitudes to-wards Islam in Europe and the United States. In Europe, "the most important factor in the resurgence of the far-right move-ments is their ability to present Islam as an unyielding force, in-capable of being assimilated into the national culture, by emphasizing both the fragility and the importance of European cultural values ... The American perception of Islam, in contrast, is largely based on a form of externalization tied to foreign policy and the troubles in the Middle East ... Hostility is less the result of competing national identities and more something that stems from the constant redefinition of and shifting balance between ethnic groups" (Cesari 2004a, 31, 32). In both cases, Islam is as-sociated with fanaticism but the danger it presents is different: the troubles in the Middle East impinge on the US economic and political interests while Islam in Europe has more to do with identity or symbolic interests.

However, in some if not most situations, the distinction may not be very clear. As Zolberg and Woon (1999, 8) point out, negotiations on how to deal with cultural differences involve difficult questions. Indeed, although the most important aspects of culture pertain to meaning and fundamental beliefs and ideas about existence, they are embedded in organizations with their rules, procedures, and modes of communication. In other words, controversies and negotiations over issues involving fundamental beliefs and ideas regarding existence can be direct and indirect: the first are about the ideological differences themselves while the second are about specific issues as surrogates for ideological differences (Brown and Brown 1983, 235–6). Debates over the Muslim veil may be an instance of indirect negotiations: it is not the veil as such that is the issue, but the cultural and value differences that it symbolizes. This possibility was noted in some case studies discussed in the previous chapter (Germain 2004; Isin and Siemiatycki 2002).

Negotiations are more likely to be successful if the issues are defined in terms of practical arrangements rather than matters of fundamental principles. Indeed, "ideological negotiations" are more subject to misunderstandings and distortions due to differences in perceptions and evaluations of the merit of the various options, and they are subject to emotional polarization because of the perceived threat to the group (Brown and Brown 1983, 236).

To the extent that negotiations are about practical arrangements, they might be more likely to succeed at the local than at the regional and national levels. Arrangements may be more easily devised within the context of a limited number of specific circumstances. In contrast, the negotiation of suitable arrangements in large, highly complex and diversified environments such as metropolitan areas, regions, and entire countries would tend to be more difficult. Contacts between institutional agents and community representatives would tend to be established more easily at the local than at the higher levels of socio-political organization. In addition, social experimentation and incremental change may perhaps be more possible at the local level than at the level of the larger society. There is also the possibility that successfully negotiated arrangements in one local community may influence other communities to proceed or may serve as examples (Cesari 2004a, 132). These are all hypotheses to be examined empirically.

THE RELEVANCE OF THE FORMS
AND CULTURE OF PUBLIC INSTITUTIONS

Several important *cultural values* come into play in the negotiations over cultural and religious issues. Foremost among them are the generally accepted and legally established covenants of human rights, in particular, those pertaining to freedom of religious expression. Hypothetically, religious freedom as a cultural value would facilitate accommodations. It would be a necessary but not a sufficient condition for successful incorporation of religious minorities. It has been suggested, for example, that resistance from non-Muslims to the building of Islamic cultural centres is less pronounced in the United States than in Europe – at least it was before September 2001 – largely "because religious freedom and the social role of religion is seen as one of the cornerstones of American society" (Cesari 2004, 135). But the events of September 11, the international situation, and the related foreign policy may have changed public attitudes.

However, different conceptions of religion can lead to different expectations of what is meant by "freedom of religion" (Sander 1991, 66). In Sweden, for example, the legislation is based "on the distinction between a sacred/religious and a secular/profane sphere, assuming that the first is concerned only with private matters ... problems of individual and private moral sentiment and behaviour, solutions to problems of the meaning of life, salvation, etc." In the second, the secular sphere, all are equal and must follow the same laws, rules and basic cultural norms, irrespective of religious beliefs and affiliations (65).

That is, freedom of religious expression is to occur within an individualist, subjectivist, and segmented conception of religion. In contrast, religion can be seen as orienting and regulating all or a significant range of aspects of daily life. This is the approach in religions that contain rules on matters such as dress, marriage, divorce, custody of children, inheritance, and the slaughter of animals.

When these two conceptions of freedom of religion, whether incorporated in legislation (as in Sweden) or simply entrenched in the culture, come into conflict, it may be difficult to pursue successful negotiations. "Many of the problems that Muslims in Sweden are facing can be largely attributed to the notion, nature and place of religion in our society which includes the notion that it should not be allowed to affect your behaviour outside your very private sphere" (Sander 1991, 67).

There is a conflict between the view of the state as a secular institution and as one that embodies the norms and values of a particular religion. The state as a secular institution constitutes a cultural framework that is likely to shape the evolution of negotiations between governmental organizations and religious groups. The existence of religious pluralism in a society supports – and may even require – that state institutions, though rooted in a value system, should be secular. Indeed, if the state were to be associated with a particular religion, with what religion would it be associated? However, as will be seen later, the existence of an established church may sometimes facilitate the accommodation of minority religions.

So, on the one hand there is religious freedom and the pressures for recognition on the part of particular groups, but, on the other hand, religious pluralism sets serious constraints on the recognition of any one religion. This is perhaps one reason why institutional arrangements in most countries today seem to be based on three principles: individual freedom of religion, even-handedness vis-à-vis religious communities, and a selective co-operation with formally or informally recognized religious organizations (Koenig 2005a, 4).

Wuthnow (1994, 8) notes that the most literal meaning of *public* is the people. This is relevant in the present context because the focus is on religion in its collective manifestations and influences rather than on its individual expressions. In other words, the elements that are considered are the expressions of religion that are widespread and that involve people's collective identity as a people. In situations of religious pluralism, it would seem that the relevant public consists of the members of a particular religious community, and not the public at large. Thus religious freedom would explain why immigrants gravitate to their own churches (Hurh and Kim 1990, 32). State secularism and religious pluralism would act in such a way as to make their specific religious communities the only relevant one for the public expressions of religion.

Among the cultural values embedded in the structure of public institution and in their constitutional and legal underpinnings, a number are relevant in this context. Governmental bodies at the local, regional, and national levels, churches and religious organizations, human rights organizations, the media, and universities are all driven to a certain extent by a body of values and norms. Not all of these values may involved in each public confrontation, but they may, in one case or another, be relevant for the evolution and outcome of a controversy.

SOME CROSS-NATIONAL COMPARISONS

Some cross-national comparisons can be fruitful for the formulation of hypotheses about the influence of the structure and value orientations of public institutions on the processes by which religious minorities and their institutions are incorporated into the society. The comparative analyses of European countries found in the research literature show that interesting differences in institutional structures and traditions have led countries to adopt different strategies for the institutional integration of religious diversity. Although the study of European countries is beyond the scope of the present analysis,

Table 3
Muslim population in selected European countries, 2010

| | Muslims | | Total population |
	Percentage	Millions	Millions
France	9.7	6.12	62.67
Germany	5.2	4.28	82.09
Netherlands	5.8	0.96	16.66
Great Britain	4.0	2.47	61.89
Norway	1.8	0.09	4.85
Sweden	5.5	0.52	9.29
Denmark	3.9	0.02	5.48

Source: Kettani (2010).

a brief overview of the experience of some of the countries included in a number of comparative analyses will be presented later in the chapter.

The overview begins with some background information on those countries starting with a few statistics on their religious demography. First, of all non-Christian religious groups, Muslims constitute the largest percentage of the total population in all the countries considered in the following analysis. The other non-Christian immigrant minorities combined constitute less than 2 per cent.

Second, it is in France, the Netherlands, and Germany that their percentage is the largest. Third, even though proportions matter, absolute numbers are also important. In Canada, as shown in Table 1, both the numbers and their percentage are relatively small in comparison with the comparable figures in a number of European countries. In the United State, the percentage of Muslims is relatively small (2.5), but since the population is large, the small percentage corresponds to a large number of Muslims, that is, almost 8 million. The percentages in France, Germany, and the United Kingdom are relatively high and correspond to significant numbers of Muslims (6, 4, and almost 2.5 million, respectively).

It is difficult to assess the influence of both percentages and absolute numbers on the processes of integration, but it can be expected to be significant. Data on the geographic distribution of the religious minorities would also be needed for such an assessment. Indeed, minorities – the immigrant and second generations in particular – tend to be concentrated in cities and in certain areas within cities. When the numbers are small and dispersed, it may be possible to think of integration as a primarily individual phenomenon involving individual characteristics and attitudes. With large, concentrated numbers, however, collective processes are set in motion. As noted in chapter 2, it is necessary to consider not only interpersonal but also intergroup relations, that is, the "sense of group position" (Blumer 1958; Bobo and Hutchings 1996).

In spite of the demographic differences, a number of common features characterize the experience of most European countries. First, when the new immigration began a few decades ago, most of the immigrants considered themselves, and were considered, to be temporary sojourners, or "guest workers" – a status that is not conducive to integration into the larger society. The guestworker policy tended to prevent governments from adopting systematic integration programs. However, with time it became obvious that most "sojourners" would not be returning home and that they were in fact immigrants who would stay and eventually bring their families. This situation led to a shift toward policies of integration.

The restrictiveness of the requirements for citizenship can vary. Howard (2009) has developed a Citizenship Policy Index (CPI) based on three types of requirements. The first is whether the children born in the country automatically receive that country's citizenship. It is automatic in Canada and the United States, but several European countries impose certain conditions, usually tied to the length of legal residence of the parents. The second consists of residence requirements, that is, "the number of years before an individual immigrant can become a naturalized citizen and the time required for an immigrant who is married to a citizen "(23). There can also be "civic integration" requirements, such as mandatory language and civics tests. Finally, a country may or may not allow its citizens to hold dual citizenship.

On the basis of these elements, Howard classified fifteen European countries as restrictive, medium, or liberal. Of the eight countries, three (Denmark, Germany, and Austria) were classified as restrictive, two (the Netherlands, and Sweden) as medium, and three (Britain, Belgium, and France) as liberal. Canada and the United States can also be included in the third category. In addition, the fact that immigrants are from former colonies, as is the case in a number of European countries, can work against the process of integration (Howard 2009, 38–42). Indeed, the collective memories of the colonial experience are frequently negative for both sides, albeit for different reasons. In addition to the colonial past, there is the fact that "from the beginning of the Crusades up to the Gulf war going through the colonial epic, violence and confrontation have always, in historiographies, marked the relations between the Muslim world and Europe" (Cesari 2004b, 147, my translation).

The conflation of categories of race, class, and religion which, as noted above, is the case in a number of countries, compounds the problems of integration and the recognition of religious minorities other than the Judeo-Christian. This may not be peculiar to European countries, but is certainly occurs in a number of them. Of primary interest, however, are the features of the institutions that differ in the different countries (Koenig 2007). Indeed, divergences in public responses to demands for recognition can be explained in part by the varying institutional arrangements of political organization (Bader 2007; Koenig 2005b, 221). They are partly shaped by the inherited Church-State institutions that have oriented the political debate about the rights and practices of religious minorities (Soper and Fetzer 2007, 934).

The British institutional system of governance is decentralized. This important feature seems to facilitate negotiations between actors of civil society and the government since many take place at the local level. The decentralization of authority – and therefore the greater scope for initiative – provides room for local authorities to adapt and react to local political pressures without too much constraint by central government. The decentralization "provides political space for pressures to be placed on the structures where it matters ... At the local level the practicalities of everyday negotiations over detail, with give and take, are a major determinant in the decisions which affect the everyday life of all the community, Muslim or not" (Nielsen 1991, 52–3). Thus, successful arrangements regarding most types of claims by religious minorities are negotiated with relatively little resistance. At the national level, however, where there is much less flexibility, the level of resistance and tensions is much higher, in particular with regard to the incorporation of religious differences into the body of national symbols (Koenig 2005b, 226–7).

In addition, the existence of a formal religious establishment, the Church of England, which, on the surface might appear to be a barrier to any claims by religious minorities, has in fact served as an institutional and ideological resource for them. "Far from opposing state accommodation for religious groups, the (church-state) model makes significant allowances for it, and resources flow to religious schools and social service agencies as a consequence." In other words, the model makes allowances for state accommodation of religious groups. Thus, Anglican, Catholic, and Jewish leaders are reluctant to oppose state assistance to other religious groups since denying benefits to them would "call into question the very system that provided *them* with considerable state aid" (Soper and Fetzer 2007, 936).

On the other hand, there is no legislation that protects religious minorities *qua* religious minorities from discrimination. Rather, they are protected as ethnic or racial minorities. Thus religious groups that are ethnically homogeneous (such as Sikhs and Jews) are protected in both regards by the Race Relations Act. In their case, practices or symbols can be seen under the Act as ethnic as well as religious. But ethnically heterogeneous religious groups (such as Muslims) are not protected as religious minorities; their adherents are protected as members of ethnic or racial groups (Vertovec 1997, 177). This particularity of the legislation makes it more difficult for some religious minorities to obtain institutional recognition (Peach 2004, 181).

In France, all types of claims seem to encounter strong resistance – basically because many of the functions of government are concentrated in the central government and because of the national ideology and symbolism of secularism (*laïcité*). Religious claims are easily perceived as transgressing the symbolic boundary between the public and the private. Particularistic identities, such as religious identities, are relegated to the private sphere. Because of this secular ideology of the state, "debates take place at a level of principle in which compromise is virtually excluded in advance" or, at best, very difficult to consider (Rath et al. 2001, 4; Soper and Fetzer 2007, 937).

Another form of centralization is apparent in the fact that in France those wishing to make a rights-based argument against the state cannot have recourse to the courts. "The protection of individual and civil rights is guaranteed through legislation rather than through the application of constitutional clauses by the courts. The French administrative courts such as the Council of State and the Constitutional Council are unlike the American and Canadian Supreme Courts in that private parties cannot bring cases before these bodies" (Wayland 1997, 557). To the degree that pluralistic modes of incorporation are adopted at all, they were highly controlled by the state (Koenig, 2005b, 226–7). An illustration is the representative structure of Islam that has been set up as a result of a State initiative. With the proliferation of associations in the 1980s, Islam became an agent that had to be dealt with. Thus, in 1989, the Ministry of the Interior, wishing to have a legitimate "interlocuteur" representing the Islamic community, established a structure on which sit fifteen members representing the Muslims in their diversity (Khosrokhavar 1997, 261, 267).

In addition, although the state officially does not support religious organizations, it provides funding for public service and community groups that incorporate Islamic identity and culture into their activities. These initiatives gave greater public value to religious organizations in the eyes of the Muslim population (Kastoryano, 2004, 1238).

The French state recognizes religious communities but not "ethnies." In creating a French Muslim community, with its representatives, the French state hopes to dissociate French Islam from its foreign patrons and to establish a body it can deal with. However, this can run the risk of encouraging community formation among Arabs by strengthening the link between ethnicity and religion, a link that was becoming weaker (Roy 1992, 86). This is in contrast with Germany, where ethnicity is officially recognized. The Committee for Foreigners created by the German government finances projects of immigrant associations "judged to be of social benefit such as the salvaging of deviants, unemployed persons, delinquents ... Thus, nationality became the primary source for (Turkish) ethnicity whereas in France religion became the basis of ethnicity" (Kastoryano 2004, 1238, 1241).[1]

Germany's polity has been described as "state-corporatist" in which incorporation has, as in France, been controlled by the central state. A critical issue of incorporation has to do with the system of privileged relation between the state and religious communities. Indeed, in certain respects, Germany has an institutionalized religious plurality. A formal separation between Church and State is established by the German Basic Law. Nevertheless, the constitution provides for co-operation between the two institutions in such areas as education and social welfare. Thus, the issue is not whether the state should accommodate religion in public institutions; it already does (Soper and Fetzer 2007, 938).

Because of the federal structure of government in Germany, some policy areas are dealt with at the *Länder* level. For instance, responsibility for matters of culture and therefore also of religious education reside at that level. A further peculiarity of the German institutional arrangements is that in all *Länder*, religious education can be planned and implemented only in collaboration with, and under the responsibility of, the churches. The Christian and Jewish communities are funded through a "church tax" which the members of the particular community voluntarily pay to a representative body. With these revenues, the churches can not only cover their regular expenses but also staff and partly fund organizations that are not specifically religious but of a more general social nature (Doomernik 1995, 54–5).

Thus, the Protestant and Roman Catholic churches have well-established and legally safeguarded interests and financial resources. These are not available to Muslims since they do not have a representative body although it is possible that one may eventually be established (Karakasoglu and Nenneman 1997, 252). However, the fact that such arrangements already exists for other religions makes it easier for Muslims to demand that the state extend them to Islam. Thus the German Church-State model provides opportunities for the political mobilization of Muslim groups for the pursuit of incorporation into the existing institutional system (Soper and Fetzer 2007, 938).

The issue is whether the state will expand its religious establishment to include Islam and its institutions and how to achieve such an objective. For a number of years, several Muslim associations have in fact attempted to form legal corporations in conformity with the legal-framework parameters of the corporatist state. They sought to be recognized as Public Law Bodies in the same way as churches and synagogues (Waardenburg 1991, 35). However, no Islamic organization has been able to claim to represent the Islamic "church." This is because its "non-hierarchical, polyphonic nature does not offer up a legally recognizable authority that can receive and distribute tax support" (Alba 2005, 32). As a result, the existing modes of obtaining state funds by churches in Germany are not or not easily available to Muslims.

In the Netherlands, because of religious "pillarization,"[2] religious activities are accepted even when they reach far beyond the daily routine of prayer and enter into the political arena. "Dutch society has evolved according to the concept of living-apart-together" (Doomernik 1995, 53–4). Beginning in 1983, a constitutional amendment launched the process of "depillarization." Organizations based on religion and ideology gradually began to loose their monopolistic position; some even ceased to exist. But the process of "depillarization" is still under way (Rath et al. 2001, 260–4). The "pillars" have lost much of their ideological significance, but they still exist and operate in practice (Doomernik 1995, 53–4). Indeed, the idea of pillarization has been adopted for Islam: Muslims have the right to set up their own institutions, just as Catholics and Protestants do. The school system is organized along religious lines; Muslims have separate radio and television stations; government provides funding for the recruitment of religious leaders in other countries and provides subsidies to a range of minority organizations (Duyvené de Wit and Koopmans 2005). Accordingly, few claims by Muslims have been categorically rejected. This is partly because the claims are based on the principle of equal treatment with existing groups.

Moreover, in Dutch constitutional law, certain powers are decentralized so that they can take account of local circumstances. Nevertheless, "during negotiations, the majority often tries to steer institutionalization toward more liberal and "Dutch" practices, that is to say away from orthodoxy ... We are left with the impression that time is needed to get used to Muslim claims before granting them, with mixed feelings" (Rath et al. 2001, 263).

A "pillarization" strategy requires representative Muslim organizations. The development of such organizations was more successful at the local than at the national level as were negotiations over matters such as the building of a mosque. But there are still controversies, and those at the local level occasionally escalate to the national level (Sunier 2005, 87–88). Such controversies can be accentuated by economic recessions in part because they put a heavy financial burden on the state, a burden that many consider partly due to the extensive support to religious minorities.

The controversies are also due to events on the national and international scenes which make the accommodation of Islam more controversial. They are also due to the fact that the "de-pillarization" process is not complete; in fact, some forms of it are adopted to deal with the growing presence of Islam in the country. Sunier (2005, 95) suggests that "despite obvious parallels with the situation in other European countries, the developments in the Netherlands are uniquely 'Dutch' in many respects. This 'Dutchness' is revealed in a discourse that conflates issues of integration with 'de-pillarization' and 'de-confessionalization.'" Indeed, to the extent that "pillarization" is legally established, it may prevent or slow down the eventual integration of the religious minority by making it more difficult for members of the minority to blend into the larger society. In other words, it may serve to maintain some rigidity in the social boundaries between different segments of the society.

It seems quite clear that several features of a society's institutional system of governance influence the extent and modalities of incorporation of religious minorities. There are certainly features in addition to those mentioned that are relevant. The study of the particular institutional features of other countries would also provide additional insights. For example, in Denmark the free-school legislation entitles any group of parents over a certain number to establish their own school with public funding (Hjarno 1997, 293). In Sweden there is state support for "free church federations" above a certain size to parallel that granted to the state Lutheran church (Nielsen 1991, 51). In Norway, the state gives financial support to registered religious and philosophical societies. The size of the subsidies depends on the number of members, and at the end of the year, each group must submit a list of members and other organizational documentation in order to continue receiving the subsidies (Naguib 2002, 164).

Finally, there are a few exceptional cases: Austria passed a Law of Recognition of Islam in 1874, which was enlarged in 1912, and Belgium recognized Islam officially in 1974 (Waardenburg 1991, 38). In addition, in Belgium the salaries and pensions of the ministers of six recognized religions are paid by the state.

This brief overview of the situation in a few countries shows that the governance of religious diversity can have several facets. Koenig (2009) suggests the following classification of the modalities of governance of religious diversity. Governments can (1) define the legal status of religious communities; (2) specify at least the minimum the degree of autonomy that they will enjoy; (3) provide various amounts of financing directly through subsidies, payment of salaries, or "church taxes," for example, or indirectly through tax exemptions; (4) provide financing to faith-based education; (5) introduce or allow the inclusion of religious education in the curriculum of public schools; and (6) give financial assistance to faith-based social service agencies (whether or not there is state financing of churches).[3]

The various institutional accommodations and arrangements, however, can also be divided into two broad categories. The first consists of a system structured in such a way that individuals and sub-groups in the mainstream and in the minorities function in parallel institutions in a number of domains. In contrast, the second type of arrangement seem to be aimed primarily at facilitating the minority's community life, but the assumption is that critical participation is to take place in the context of the institutions of the larger society (for example, the school system and the media). As a result, in the first type of accommodations, much of the activities and the social relations of the different groups will tend to take place within the boundaries of their respective socio-religious communities. In the second type, there would be more activities and social relations across these social boundaries. One type would be conducive to integration while the other would tend to slow the process of integration.[4]

CHALLENGES TO THE COLLECTIVE IDENTITY AND CULTURE

Grim and Finke (2006, 8) include another type of regulation, namely, "social regulation," which refers to "restrictions placed on practice, profession, or selection of religion by other[5] religious groups, associations, or the culture at large. This form of regulation stems from the norms and culture of the larger society. It may or may not be tolerated or encouraged by the state, but it is not formally endorsed by government action. The following section deals with some of the elements that are at the base of this type of regulation.

The collective identity and religious culture that result from the distinctive historical nation-building experience of the receiving society are important factors in the recognition and incorporation of religious minorities (Koenig 2005b, 221–2). The fact that the new religious minorities (such as Muslims, Hindus, or Sikhs) that come to Western countries have come to Christian or historically Christian societies is an important factor that needs to be considered. The incorporation of culturally different groups into the society can indeed present a serious challenge for the definition of the collective identity. This is especially critical when the religion and the associated culture and traditions of the newcomers are significantly different from those of the mainstream society.

To understand the possible sources of tensions that may arise between religious groups, it is necessary to consider the ways in which Christian religions have contributed to the identity and national narrative of the mainstream. Indeed, "the ways in which Christian religions have been institutionalized and constitute, through customs and habits of thought, part of the definition of "who we are" ... defines a boundary that identifies those who are religiously "other" (Alba 2005, 32). The existing set of national symbols can be a major obstacle to the development of more pluralistic modes of incorporation. The symbols can be such that the minority religion is perceived as essentially foreign (Koenig 2005b, 228).

European identity, despite national variations, remains deeply embedded in Christian tradition in relation to which Muslim immigrants constitute a visible "other" (Zolberg and Woon 1999, 7). This is the case even when the society proclaims the secularization of its public life. To a significant extent, European culture and symbolic system have historically been shaped by Christianity. This has also been the case in Scandinavia. In Sweden, for example, the "Evangelical-Lutheran Christianity has, for almost 500 years, exercised a tremendous influence on Swedish culture and the manners and customs, norms and value systems of the Swedes, as well as their ways of thinking (Sander 1991, 63).

However, there also appear to be variations among countries in which Christianity has historically been predominant. In his study of the role of religious legacies in the recognition of group rights, Minkenberg (2008, 55) classifies the countries included in his analysis along three cultural patterns: (1) cultures with a Protestant dominance (the Scandinavian countries); (2) cultures with a historical Protestant majority and substantial Catholic minorities "where a cultural rather than political bipolarity has emerged with sub-cultural segregation" (England and the United States); and (3) cultures "with a Catholic dominance and democratic or democratizing regimes that are characterized by large political and social fissures, organic opposition, and secularist dogmas" (France, Italy, Belgium, Austria, and Ireland).

Minkenberg's (2008) analysis shows a relationship between the religious legacies of the nineteen countries studied and the recognition of group rights. These include rights outside of public institutions (for example, ritual slaughter and provisions for burials) and inside (for example, state recognition of religious schools and the right of Islamic teachers to wear the Islamic head scarf). "Predominantly Protestant countries exhibit moderate (Great Britain, Denmark)[6] to high (Sweden) levels of cultural group rights recognition whereas Catholic countries fall in the range of low (France) to moderate (Austria, Belgium) levels." Mixed Protestant cultures fall either in the moderate (Germany) and high (the Netherlands, Canada) levels of cultural rights recognition. Minkenberg also points out that from 1990 and 2002, the shift toward cultural pluralism occurred mostly in Protestant countries – regardless of their "starting point" – whereas Catholic countries have remained more static (Minkenberg 2008, 55–6).

As Shadid and van Koningsveld (1991, 235) point out, it is unlikely that important changes in the Christian fundamentals of Western societies will take place soon. The presence of Islam and other non-Christian religions will continue to challenge the traditional character of European nation-states (Sunier 2005, 92). To the extent that this is the case, it will take time before minority religions will be seen as an integral part of the culture and institutional matrix of the society, notwithstanding the stated multicultural integration objectives of Western societies. The boundary between insiders and outsiders will tend to be even more pronounced when the religious differences coincide with ethnic or racial differences. And that will be even more so if the minority religion is perceived as opposed to Western culture either because its adherents are seen as enemies or because their values, customs, and ways of life not only are different but also are seen as inimical to those in the mainstream culture.

A parallel can perhaps be drawn with what has been taking place in most Arab countries, where the national narrative tend to be interwoven with Islam. That makes it difficult for Arab Christian minorities to truly identify with the national community. Perhaps in part because of this form of *symbolic exclusion*, religious minorities often tend to apply the language of their own religion to their own ethnic boundaries (Eid 2003, 31).

A similar analysis would perhaps apply, *mutatis mutandis*, in French Quebec and English-speaking Canada. From the onset, "the religious assumptions to be tried out on Canadian soil were those of the old folk churches of Christendom, churches which in Europe were typically fortified with the status of official establishment and naturally carried the assumptions of establishment in the new world" (Grant 1977, 9). "Religious establishment ended officially in Québec with the British conquest. In other provinces its rejection became final when the clergy reserves were secularized in 1854" (12).[7]

Even though the religious-establishment principle was important in shaping the Canadian character,[8] the missionary drive had a stronger effect. This drive consisted in the belief that Christians had an obligation to extend Christendom to every part of the world. Although the Roman Catholics and Protestants were at loggerheads over a number of issues, it is the similarities between the two missionary forces that are critical in the present context. The primary missionary impulse of both was to assert the lordship of Christ over every aspect of life. Their agenda included the Christianization of the whole of Canada. This included pursuing the embodiment of their social vision in legislation and public institutions (Grant 1977, 14).[9] By the time of Confederation, the establishment principle had been abandoned. The project now was to build a popular consensus about what constituted a righteous nation, a vision that was interdenominational and assumed that Canadians shared a common Christianity (Moir 2002, 19).[10]

Even though considerable secularization has taken place in recent decades, it could be argued that this Christian background is still part of the Canadian character, although perhaps more so in certain parts of the country than in others. In Quebec, for instance, "Catholicism is still is a strong identity referent ("référence identitaire") for the French-Canadian ethnic group, according to the 2001 census" (Rousseau 2005, 439). "The place of religion in the identity construction goes beyond the clerical organization. It shapes the vision of the world, values, norms and related customs and life styles" (443).[11] The Roman Catholic Church dominated the social and political scene in French Quebec: it shaped the culture, it is embedded in the narrative of French Quebec as a people, and, accordingly, it is a critical definer of the collective identity.

Demographically, Canada remains largely a Christian society. An analysis of the 1971–2001 decennial censuses showed that although religious pluralism – as measured by the number of non-Christian religious adherents – is increasing, there are countervailing trends that support continued Christian dominance (Beyer 2005).

As already noted, several changes have taken place in the sphere of religion in Canada (although they began sooner in English-speaking Canada than in Quebec). A considerable degree of secularization has taken place; the privatization of religion has gone a long way; religious practice has declined; and religion and religious authority are largely separated from the public sphere. It could be hypothesized that, accompanying these changes, a process of collective-identity reconstitution has been going on, a process in which religion is becoming secondary, if not entirely absent. A positive forecast is that what is likely to emerge is "an open attitude that will welcome religion when it can contribute to a search for meaning, and that will welcome any form of religion that promises to contribute to that search" (Grant 1977, 19).

What seems to be happening is a dissociation of religion from nationality. It has been suggested that the strong negative reactions to the public display of Islamic or other religious symbols and the accompanying requests for accommodations have been based on the feeling, among others, that "we have moved away from religion in public life; we are not ready to see it appear again" (see, for example, Germain 2004, 440, quoted above). If this is the case, it would parallel the dissociation, discussed in an earlier chapter, of religion from ethnicity and nationality among religious minorities.

Transformations towards greater inclusiveness of the "national narrative" and of the collective identity and character in any societal context (North American or European) can only take place over generations. In the meantime, the significant presence of new religions and cultures can generate considerable identity and cultural anxiety in the receiving society although not necessarily to the same degree in all national communities or their subgroups.

The anxiety can manifest itself in different ways. For example, the immigration of certain groups may be perceived as an "invasion" that would result in a "takeover" of the societal institutions. Some may fear that the behaviour of extremists in different parts of the world may be imported in their country and that these extremists will attempt to "take over the institutions of our society." This will be particularly the case if certain subgroups among them make claims on the institutions of the society and, as a result, appear to want to change the society rather than integrate into it. Public authorities and different groups will then be pressured to take measures to protect its integrity and assure its maintenance. In such a context, making small accommodations to different cultural and religious practices can be perceived as a serious threat to the society's identity, culture, and institutions.[12] Attempting to be an open and receptive society may then appear as a utopian project.

However, it is possible that the promotion and pursuit of equality of opportunity and of non-discrimination will eventually result in the upward mobility of minorities. Their growing presence in the middle class and in the upper levels of public and private organizations and in the professions would project, especially among the young, a new image of the society. Gradually, individuals may come to think of "their" society and its defining characteristics differently than did previous generations.

Some societies may be more vulnerable, at least at a particular point in their historical evolution. For example, Quebec is a society that has experienced rapid social change: a dramatic rise in the level of education, economic development, political affirmation, and extensive secularization. Globalization and especially the prevailing language and culture in North America can generate a strong sense of vulnerability in some segments of the society. The growing presence of immigrants of a different culture and religion can accentuate the collective anxiety about the national identity. For similar or different reasons, the perception of a threatened collective identity can and does occur in other societies. Comparative research on this topic is clearly needed. It is a phenomenon that is critical for the integration of immigrants.

Clearly, how cultures and collective identities change is an important object of study. Some avenues of exploration are suggested by the research reviewed. First, there is anecdotal evidence of dialogue among minority religious organizations and between them and those of mainstream society. Such inter-church contacts, especially if they are aimed at finding doctrinal commonalities, could have a significant influence on the evolution of the Canadian identity. Empirical research (in the form of case studies or otherwise) would be useful for finding out the kinds of effects that inter-church (and inter-group, generally) dialogue has, if any, on the multicultural conception of Canadian society.

Second, the multiplication of negotiated arrangements that incorporate minority religions is likely, over time, to affect the conception that people have of the character of their society. As new generations are brought up in religiously diverse surroundings, both demographically and institutionally, the way in which they view their country and nation is likely to be different from that of their ancestors. In the study of this evolution, it will be important to pay attention to how religious, ethnic, and racial diversity is incorporated into the collective imagination.

Third, the role of public education in shaping the way people think of their society is crucial. For instance, it will be fruitful to study the impact in this regard of the new religious curriculum in Quebec public schools – a curriculum consisting of courses on the great world religious traditions.

Fourth, it will be important to study the debates on the incorporation of minority religions (Rath et al. 2001, 16). What kinds of arguments are used on each side of the debate? What philosophical principles are invoked? Which interpretations of the legislation are put forward? What benefits and dangers for society are identified? What images of the ideal society underlie the perspectives of each side?

The "episode and discourse" framework developed by Moaddel (2005) for the study of phenomena such as the origins of Islamic modernism and Arab nationalism (in countries such as Egypt, India, and Iran) would be useful. In this model, the production and dissemination of socio-political ideas is seen as "an outcome of debates, contrasting positions, conflict, and disagreements over a relatively small set of issues." It is a discontinuous process that proceeds in an episodic fashion in the sense that "the setting for cultural change was structured by dramatic events or a conjuncture of historical events that interrupted the continuity of social life. These events had substantial impacts on the worldviews of cultural producers ... and contributed to the generation of a new awareness and provoked an alternative way of thinking about socio-political issues among intellectual leaders" (Moaddel 2005, 322).

CONCLUSION

Controversies seem to occur because some individuals or groups in the mainstream society feel that the identity and culture of their own community are threatened. Political and cultural elites, who generally have access to the media, can play an important role in either alleviating or exacerbating those anxieties and in indirectly supporting public manifestations of hostilities or fostering accommodating attitudes.

In several cases, accommodations have been made. And it seems that the successful ones have taken place at the level of day-to-day interaction and on a case-by-case basis. Individual schools, hospitals, community agencies, and so on do not necessarily have a grand plan for dealing with newcomers. Pragmatism leads them to apply their professional skills and norms when dealing with individual students, parents, patients, and clients, whatever the challenge they present. In other words, it seems that in many cases, pragmatism prevailed.

The effective negotiation of arrangements may not take place with equal ease or difficulty in all types of organizations. Research is needed on the variations across organizations such as schools, colleges, factories, health care organizations, and community associations.

However, public controversies that involve more complex and organized processes of negotiations do occur. It seems that a central difference has to do with the framing of the issues: in terms of practical arrangements versus issues of identity and basic principles. Negotiations appear more likely to be successful if the issues are framed in terms of the former rather than of the latter. Some of the research reviewed also suggests the possibility that accommodations would be more likely to succeed at the local than at the regional and national levels.

Also critical is the structure of public institutions, such as constitutional and legal provisions, government bodies, and human-rights organizations. A brief overview of relevant institutions and their embedded culture in European countries revealed interesting variations and their possible impact on negotiations and the resulting accommodations.

Conclusion

The analysis presented in this book is based on the research literature on religious minorities and their integration into the larger society. It has dealt mostly with the Canadian and American literature, although some European research was included. Thus the patterns observed may be applicable to most Western countries and not only to Canada and the United States.

In its analysis of newcomers and their descendants, the review focused on their religious identities, values, practices, and the evolution of the role that religion plays in their lives. It also dealt with minority religious institutions and how their role changes progressively from what it was when first established in the new society. To some extent, their doctrines, rituals, practices, behavioural prescriptions, and organizational structures are modified over time.

Similarly, the identities, social attachments, and values of the individual members of the mainstream society change in response to the growing religious pluralism. It is not possible for a community that incorporates large numbers of newcomers, especially if they belong to different cultures and religious traditions, not to be transformed to some degree. Societal institutions whose responsibilities bring them into contact with the new religious groups frequently need to modify their rules and programs to respond adequately to the newcomers. The collective identity of the receiving society also evolves so as to absorb new cultural groups.

Two basic propositions stated in the introduction are largely supported by the research literature reviewed: that the integration of immigrants and their descendants into a society is interactive and mutual and that both the new ethno-religious community and the established community change as a result of the interaction of their members and their respective groups and organizations. Progressive change as a result of their contacts is the basic significance of the notion of integration.

The research literature also supports the view that the evolution of both communities is inevitable. It may be resisted by individuals or subgroups on either side, sometimes quite strongly. That resistance may affect the pace and direction of the evolution, but it will not prevent it from happening although the different categories of immigrants may not integrate at the same pace. The past evolution of Canadian society in its relations with immigrants and their descendants is quite convincing in this regard. The Canada in which we now live is quite different than the one that existed in the 1950s or earlier. Such an evolution will continue with the increasing presence of new religious groups. Similarly, the descendants of immigrants who came to Canada in the early years of the last century are quite different from their ancestors in their self-concepts and culture.

Most of the integration takes place at the level of day-to-day interactions and accommodations. Changes in ideas, customs, lifestyles, organizational practices, and collective identity evolve out of the experiences and accommodations of everyday life. Barely noticeable modifications of ideas and ways of doing things accumulate over time. Although public policies and programs may have an impact in legitimizing new approaches, it is not at that level that integration takes place, but rather at the level of people-to-people contacts in neighbourhoods, in schools, at work, in various organizations, and in informal encounters.

This does not mean that the process of integration is always free of tensions and conflicts. The mutual adaptations do not come automatically and may encounter serious obstacles. There are individuals or groups who attempt to avoid as much as possible contacts with those who are different. Marginality – social, economic, and political – resulting from prejudice and discrimination may prevent or seriously slow down the progress of integration. Roadblocks tend to be more frequent and more serious when religious and racial differences coincide.

The analysis is briefly summarized below. It suggests a number of perspectives and points to several basic hypotheses about the role of religion for immigrants and their descendants and the relationship between religious minorities and the mainstream society. It reveals that there are several dimensions to the evolution of the religious minorities and of the receiving society; that several social processes are involved; and that the evolution follows somewhat different paths as the life circumstances of individuals and subgroups change with time and as a result of increasing contacts between the different communities. It also identifies several issues in need of further research.

THE SOCIAL AND CULTURAL
TRANSPLANTATION EXPERIENCE

It was seen that religion can play a significant role in helping newcomers cope with the crucial experience of being uprooted from one social world and transplanted into another. It can provide significant resources to help newcomers cope with the cultural disorientation, identity insecurity, and loss of control over their lives that the transplantation entails. By their very nature, religion and religious organizations are perhaps the community organizations best suited to provide the *symbolic* resources that immigrants can draw upon to cope with the transplantation experience. Indeed, religion includes a system of values and meanings and a normative framework that can be a cultural and psychological anchorage for individuals and families. But individuals and families can also find *social* assistance in the religious organizations (that is, churches and associations) of their community.

However, there is no doubt considerable variation in the extent to which and in the ways in which religion and religious organizations play a role in the lives of immigrants. There can be variations in the rapidity and in the patterns of integration. Variations may occur among and within the various religious minorities: there may be variations within a particular religion between those of different traditions (such as Muslim Sunnis and Shiites), ethnic background, and country or region of origin; between women and men, across levels of education, and between those with different degrees of religious commitment *before* they migrated to this continent.

Because religion and religious organizations are embedded in a culture, those of the ethnic community tend to be more effective than those of the mainstream society in playing this supportive role. This is, of course, especially the case when the religion of the newcomers is different from that of the receiving society. But with the progressive acculturation of individuals as they learn to cope with the requirements of their new social, cultural, and institutional environment, the relationship with their own religion and religious organizations evolves and may even be abandoned.

The extent and nature of the relationship between religious organizations and their adherents and the extent to which they are involved in the organizational or associational life of the community are not the same in all ethnic and religious groups or in all localities. There appears to be a great need for research on the variation in community involvement of minority religious organizations and the factors that could account for the variations.

SOCIAL MARGINALITY

The process of establishing roots in the society of adoption may meet some resistance and even opposition, which, in turn, would lead to social marginalization for certain subgroups of immigrants and their descendants. For members of the receiving society, the absorption of the newcomers may be seen as a threat to the collective identity, way of life, social cohesion, and organizational practices. Of course, there may be variations in the reaction to newcomers in different part of the country (for example, in metropolitan centres as opposed to small communities), in different regions and social classes.

There may be a natural reluctance to accept newcomers on the part of the "established" members of a community or society. The reluctance is accentuated when the newcomers' culture is considered inferior to or incompatible with that of the established community. Not surprisingly, the social distance and failures of integration that may result seem to occur primarily when religious affiliation is associated with a racial difference. Such reluctance may or may not result in discrimination, but if it does, it represents a serious obstacle to integration. Threatening events on the national or international scene may also increase the social distance between the receiving society and particular groups of newcomers. But the influence of such events on opinions and attitudes appears to be mostly indirect in the sense that it depends to a considerable degree on the way in which they are reported and interpreted by public authorities and the media.

Among members of religious minorities, there may be different reactions to experiences of social distance and especially of exclusion. There may be an increase in the salience of religion, subjectively and as a social "marker" and a retreat into the ethno-religious community. This may seem paradoxical, but a negative perception of one's group frequently tends to accentuate the importance of the groups for the individual and the social cohesion of the group. Of course, some will try to distance themselves from their community in order to avoid derogatory experiences. In other words, it is possible that negative experiences will result in attempts to integrate as quickly as possible into the mainstream but a the cost of rejecting one's religious and cultural background.

It is also possible that the outcome will be the emergence of a religiously based culture of opposition. Some segments of the minority religious community may respond to experiences of social exclusion and hostility by rejecting the larger society. They may adopt a paradigm of *resistance* (and opposition) based on attitudes of non-acceptance by significant members of the mainstream society. This is clearly a situation that contains the potential for conflict.

THE DISSOCIATION OF ETHNICITY AND RELIGION

After the initial transplantation stage – and perhaps beginning at that stage – the increasing interaction with individuals, groups, and institutions of the mainstream society brings about further changes in the religious identity, beliefs, normative prescriptions, and practices among members of the religious minorities. As noted by Bramadat (2005), religious doctrines, rituals, symbols, and institutions are creatively redeployed in a way that fits the new social and cultural environment. Uncertainties are experienced and new perspectives are adopted with regard to their religious heritage.

One area of questioning by members of a religious group has to do with elements of the culture that are properly religious and those that derive from their ethnic or national background. There are several circumstances that can lead to the experience of "cognitive dissonance" in the process of reconciling the patterns of behaviour expected by their religion and those expected in the host society. The dissociation of religion and ethnicity constitutes one way of dealing with the dissonance.

One such circumstance is the religious, moral, and lifestyle pluralism of North America and of Canadian society in particular. Regular encounters with people of different religious and cultural backgrounds may lead to questions about what is properly religious and what is not. Perhaps even more critical would be regular contacts with people of the same religion but of a different ethnic background. The universalistic character of the religion may contrast seriously with the particularism of the ethnic cultures. Major religions are meant to have universal relevance and applicability whereas ethnic cultures are supposed to have significance for particular people. This may become apparent to individuals as they encounter adherents of their own religion but of a different ethnicity or nationality.

The process of "negotiation" between immigrants and their children can also make individuals sensitive to what is religious and what is cultural. Such sensitivity may be more pronounced among women. Indeed, conceptions of gender roles and the related prescriptions are frequently sanctioned by the religion. The rejection of the inequality that often stems from these prescriptions could be a force leading to the view that gender roles are defined by the ethnic culture and not by the religious doctrine.

In a number of instances, the dissociation between religion and ethnicity may not be apparent because the church is seen and experienced primarily as an ethno-cultural rather than a religious milieu. Attendance is motivated primarily by the opportunity to socialize with members of one's ethnic group after services or in church-organized activities.

It should be emphasized that the blending or dissociation of religion and ethnicity is a question of degree. The two may never be completely intertwined or dissociated, either in the mind of individual adherents or in the perceptions of outside observers. Certain moral prescriptions, practices, or rituals may be specific to a particular ethnic group; conversely an ethnic group may incorporate into its cultures elements that stem from the religion to which most of its members have historically adhered.

Finally, the fact that many members of minorities progressively dissociate their religion from their ethnicity does not mean that their religion is lived outside a cultural context. Rather it is progressively embedded in the Canadian, Western culture. A new blending emerges in which elements of the mainstream culture, secular and religious, become incorporated into the doctrine, moral values and norms, and practices of the religious minority. In other words, to a certain extent, the secular and the sacred always tend to be intertwined and to shape one another. Religion does not exist in a demographic, social, economic, and cultural vacuum.

CHANGES IN RELIGIOUS ATTITUDES AND PRACTICES

Another area of questioning and creative adaptation brought about by increasing interaction with the mainstream society concerns the relevance, when situated in a new social and cultural context, of the religious doctrines, rituals, symbols, and institutions that minorities bring with them. There are features of the new context, such as secularization and religious pluralism, which can lead members of minorities to question their religious allegiances and participation. In other words, there may be a decline of religion as a basis of social identity and community attachments. This may lead some to abandon their traditional religious culture and practices.

One factor in this regard pertains to the capacity of the minority community to impose conformity to its norms and role specifications. In a large urban environment, individual behaviour is less and less subject to surveillance by others in the religious community and accordingly individuals have more opportunities to improvise on and deviate from communal expectations. The degree to which an individual's behaviour is observable would depend, among other things, on the degree of residential segregation of the group and on where the individuals study, work, and socialize.

In fact, the patterns observed in the mainstream society with regard to the place of religion in one's life, such as the importance attached to religion and religious practice, seem to be progressively adopted by members of religious minorities. And as observed among mainstream individuals, members of minorities also seem to move towards a private practice of their religion (as opposed to church attendance). Gans's (1994) hypothesis that religiosity is becoming increasingly "symbolic" may apply to some members of minorities as well as of the mainstream.

In short, there is evidence that religious acculturation is progressively taking place. The empirical evidence suggests that the patterns that emerge over time and generations with regard to religiosity and practice in religious minorities tend to progressively mirror those that have come to prevail in recent decades in the mainstream society. As a result, the same variations in religiosity and practices would eventually be observed among minorities as in the larger society.

However, some studies suggest, at least hypothetically, that the process of change towards modernity begins in the country of origin and that the evolution undergone by Western societies has been taking place for some time in the non-Western countries from which most immigrants now come. This is a matter that needs further exploration because it may be a significant factor in the process of acculturation in certain religious groups or subgroups.

THE EVOLUTION OF MINORITY RELIGIOUS INSTITUTIONS

Minority religious institutions are also affected by the interaction of their members with the mainstream society and its institutions. Indeed, members of the minority need assistance in coping with the day-to-day requirements of functioning in the new society. This frequently leads to their progressive integration into the mainstream, and that may eventually make some of them less interested in participating in the religious organizations of their own community. As a result of their interaction with the larger society, members of the minority may feel they need to address the "dissonance" between their doctrines, moral prescriptions, rituals, and the religious practices and features of the new social and cultural environment.

One way in which religious organizations can remain relevant for community members and ensure their continued participation is to help them with the problems of integration. Assistance can take many forms: the provision of practical services, such as help with finding housing or dealing with governmental agencies, making opportunities available for the acquisition of useful skills, and making cultural tools available for coping with the moral challenges encountered in the new cultural milieu.

Minority religious organizations may also become agents of acculturation by offering a paradigm through which the new society is defined and interpreted. Specifically, the diffusion of the *embrace* and *selective engagement paradigm* would lead to the blurring of social boundaries between various groups in the society and, as a result, contribute to acculturation and integration of newcomers. The extent to which this actually occurs is difficult to assess. The body of research pertaining to the relationship between religion and prejudice suggests that religion often reinforces rather than blurs social boundaries. But this research does not describe an entirely negative situation. Some results presented above suggest that some churches do orient their adherents to the well-being of the larger society and away from an exclusive concern with their own community.

Pressures are felt by leaders for the reinterpretation of traditional doctrines and normative prescriptions in such a way that they make sense in the new environment. Such reinterpretations might be a fruitful area of research. What kinds of adaptations to the new cultural environment are made? Do they involve an exploration of the original sacred texts, borrowing from other religions, or the search for a justification for a particular change?

Pressures for adapting liturgical practices, leadership roles, and other features of organizational functioning are also likely to be felt. This is particularly the case when the minority religion is not culturally and institutionally established in the adopted society. Four areas of transformation undertaken by religious organizations in response to the demands of the cultural environment and of the constantly changing situations in which find themselves have been explored: (1) changes in organizational structure and roles; (2) modification of the religious ideas, symbols, and practices; (3) attempts to be more inclusive and, as a result, becoming multi-ethnic and (4) a shift in the relative importance of religious and secular organizations in the functioning and governance of the community as a result of the religious evolution of individuals and a related decline in the influence of religious leaders.

THE PURSUIT OF SOCIAL AND INSTITUTIONAL RECOGNITION BY THE NEW MINORITIES

Integration is a process that involves not only individuals but organizations as well. New religious communities aspire to have their institutions established in the new society. They seek to be recognized by the institutions of the larger society. This can take many forms, but whatever the form, the mainstream society and its institutions are pressured to respond to the needs and demands of newcomers. And the more the new religious groups are culturally different from the mainstream, the greater the challenge of responding to their presence and their cultural specificity.

A first and important question in this regard concerns the extent to which religious minorities exert pressure for recognition and incorporation into the institutional matrix of the society. A second related question pertains to the forms of recognition that are sought. Three sets of issues were considered in this connection: (1) the types of claims made by religious minorities and their articulation; (2) the extent of support from members of the religious minority; and (3) patterns of controversies and their resolution.

It was found that although some communities or subgroups within the communities do attempt to exert pressures on public institutions, this does not seem to be a general pattern. Peaceful coexistence seems to be the desired goal. However, to the extent that it does take place, the search for a public recognition has been found to generate tensions and confrontations between the minority religious groups and those in the mainstream community who resist such recognition and accommodation.

CONDITIONS AND PROCESSES OF INCORPORATION

Controversies seem to occur because some individuals or groups in the mainstream society feel that the identity and culture of their own community is threatened. As noted earlier, the identity and culture of the receiving society will gradually change if the number of newcomers is proportionately large. The fact that change is inevitable does not mean that it does not generate considerable identity and cultural anxiety in the receiving society, anxiety that is somewhat parallel to the identity and cultural anxiety experienced by those who are transplanted into a new society. The perceptions of a threat to one's identity and culture may also lead to conflict. And insofar as the claims for recognition are seen as a threat to the predominantly Christian character of the society or to a collective identity that includes both religious and secular (or humanistic) elements, the conflict will include some definition of the "other" at least partly in religious terms.

As some studies have shown, political and cultural elites, who generally have access to the media, can play an important role in exacerbating those anxieties and the perceptions of a threat in the public. Their public statements and the images they publicize of certain groups can have a polarizing effect on inter-group relations by accentuating "us against them" perceptions and the feelings of marginality among minorities.

But they can also be such as to discourage public manifestations of hostilities and even foster accommodating attitudes. Indeed, even though the possibility of conflict may have been present, it seems that, in a number of cases, accommodations have been made and issues have been negotiated. However, it seems that much of the recognition and accommodation that have been somewhat successful have been "negotiated" at the level of day-to-day interaction on a case-by-case basis. Particular schools, hospitals, community agencies, and so on do not necessarily have a grand plan for dealing with newcomers. However, pragmatism leads them to apply their professional skills and norms when dealing with individual students, parents, patients, and clients, whatever the challenge they present. Creative modifications or applications of ideas and practices are adopted to deal with the requirements of the situation.

In other words, it seems that pragmatism has often prevailed. Several conditions may facilitate pragmatic approaches in situations of inter-group contacts. For instance, on both sides, enough people and especially social leaders may realize that the changing demographic, social, and cultural environment cannot be wished away: the school has to function, the hospital must deal with patients, the athletic team needs to train so as to win the game, public services need to be provided, and so on. There may be a realization that the cost of avoiding such changes could be quite high both for the practitioners themselves, their organization, and for the community. Accordingly, a pragmatic approach leads them to modify their ways of thinking and behaving as they encounter new circumstances. This is partly because many environments in which people function consist of a "social organization based on roles rather than persons" (Coleman 1970, 163); among other things, that means that "continuity of obligation resides in the role, rather than the person" (164).

The effective negotiation of arrangements may not take place with equal ease or difficulty in all types of organizations. It may vary across organizations such as schools, colleges, factories, health care institutions, social assistance agencies, athletic organizations, religious organizations, and community associations.

The fact that the performance of individuals tends to be evaluated in terms of role requirements and objectives does not mean, however, that the characteristics of persons have no effect on organizational relationships. Here again, prejudice against certain groups – ethno-religious and racial – may slow down and even prevent the social negotiation of workable arrangements and practices. This is suggested, for instance, by the demand for schools specifically for Black students.

The pragmatic negotiation of arrangements presupposes, of course, that certain categories of individuals are not simply excluded from becoming participants. By law, such exclusion may not take place in public institutions, but it may in other kinds of institutions.

From time to time, public controversies involve more complex and organized processes of negotiations. It seems that a central reason is the framing of the issues. Negotiations appear more likely to succeed if the issues are framed in terms of practical arrangements rather than questions of identity and fundamental principles. It also seems that accommodations are more likely to succeed at the local than at the regional and national levels.

However, there are also important *cultural values* that come into play in the negotiations between religious minorities and mainstream groups and institutions. Some are generally accepted, such as the established human rights codes, which include freedom of religious expression. Such a basic principle would be a necessary but not sufficient condition for successful accommodation.

Also critical is the structure of authority in public institutions, that is, the constitutional and legal framework within which they operate. The organizational culture that defines existing social expectations and patterns of behaviour is also important. A brief overview of relevant institutions in European countries revealed interesting variations in the structure and culture of public institutions and their impact on negotiations and the resulting accommodations. For instance, it was noted that some institutional arrangements favour the formation of parallel institutions. That is, the system is structured in such a way that individuals and subgroups in the mainstream and in the minority communities function in parallel institutions in a number of domains. On the other hand, some arrangements that seem to be aimed primarily at facilitating the minority's community life assume that critical participation is to take place in the institutions of the larger society. Thus one type of arrangement encourages activities and social relations within the boundaries of the various socio-religious communities, whereas the other favours the pursuit of activities and the formation of social relations across these social boundaries. One type would be conducive to integration while the other would tend to slow the process of integration.

Finally, what may sometimes be overlooked because of the secularist trend in Western culture is the fact that the new religious minorities (such as Muslim, Hindus, and Sikhs) come to societies whose culture derive from a largely Judeo-Christian history. In addition, the conceptions that the host society has of itself and of the ways in which it should be organized and function can clash with those of newcomers. The incorporation of groups whose religious and secular cultures are different can also bring about controversies within the mainstream society about the redefinition of the society's culture and identity and about conceptions of its social and political organization.

Some internal contradictions or confusion in the host society can also come to the surface in the process of integrating newcomers. Milot (2009, 124) observes great confusion between the secularization of political structures and individual freedom of expression; and between the notion of state neutrality and the accommodation of religious expressions. Certain segments of the population seem to assume that the secular nature of public institutions must also apply to individuals and that signs of religious affiliation have no place in the public sphere. She also notes that "in fact, the explicit desire to "laicize" the public sphere in many countries has often concealed an implicit expectation that the public expression of religious affiliation would be tolerated only when it approximated the way the majority of community members expressed their religiosity."

The basic hypothesis suggested by the research literature is that both the incoming groups and the mainstream evolve in these ways over more or less long periods of time. To paraphrase Bramadat's (2005, 13–14) proposition about incoming religious minorities and apply it to the larger society, one could say that the culture incorporated in the main symbols, institutions, and conceptions of the mainstream society are redeployed in a uniquely Canadian way. Such a re-creation happens neither *in toto* nor *ex nihilo;* rather, the mainstream remakes its culture and identity out of a combination of old and new building resources.

Finally, institutional recognition may not by itself eliminate social and cultural marginality. Peach (2004) points out that even if a minority religion is recognized in the larger society, social marginality may nevertheless be experienced by its adherents. Hypothetically, institutional accommodations could affect attitudes in the population and, as a result, facilitate the integration of newcomers. But the marginality associated with socio-economic inequalities is not likely to be overcome by the institutional recognition of the religion. Other measures would clearly be required to overcome such marginality.

Of course, the existing research literature is not final. It contains a large array of hypotheses and findings. However, it is important to emphasize that considerable research is needed in all the areas examined. One of the questions that needs further exploration is whether the factors and processes involved in the integration of minorities are the same when the religion is the same as that of the mainstream society as when it is different. Several

results presented at different points in the analysis suggest that
integration follows similar patterns. However, no systematic
comparative analyses have been found on this question.

Herberg (1960, 27–8) pointed out several years ago that integration into the new society entailed giving up virtually every-
thing brought from the "old country" (language, nationality,
and way of life) but it "did not involve abandoning the old religion. Quite the contrary, the shape of America was such that it
was largely in and through their religion that immigrants, or
rather their children and grandchildren, found their place in the
society.[1] This was the case in large part because earlier immigrants were primarily people within the Judeo-Christian tradition: Protestantism, Catholicism, and Judaism. Their religion
"fitted" in the context of the "established" Christian religion of
their new country.

However, it seems that the numerically significant immigration
of individuals of non-Christian religions coming to a society in
which their own religion is not culturally and institutionally established brings about a new challenge for both the new ethno-
religious groups and the mainstream society. The challenge
consists in institutional recognition, and the socio-cultural integration of non-Christian religions into a primarily and historically
Christian society offers particular challenges. Christian churches
and organizations had to make accommodations for their immigrant newcomers (for example, in the language of sermons and
the adoption of certain rituals brought from the country of origin), but as the research reviewed indicates, the accommodations
frequently involve more significant innovations.

A fair amount of research has been carried out on tensions and
controversies between minority religious groups and the larger society. The studies include many interesting findings and suggest
further hypotheses to be explored. However, additional research is
needed on the interaction – exchanges, collaboration, and conflicts
– between groups within religious traditions, between minorities,
and between minorities and the larger society and its institutions.

Indeed, little systematic research seems to exist on the tensions, controversies, and conflicts and on the accommodations

worked out between groups within religious congregations, between adherents to different traditions of the same religion, or between ethnic, racial, or national subgroups of the same religion. More needs to be known on the dynamics of the controversies and conflicts that emerge in different circumstances. For instance, subgroups and leaders may have conflicting ideas "about how this heterogeneous population should be brought together to form a single community behind one or other leader or 'spokesman'" (Kepel (1997, 50). On the positive side, attempts at collaboration and mutual understanding[2] between religious communities or between subgroups within a community should be examined empirically.

More also needs to be known about the variations according to gender, age, generation, and socio-economic status; between religions, and among the various traditions within the same religion. All subgroups do not encounter the same opportunities and obstacles in their pursuit of integration and accommodations. As Kepel (1997, 50) points out, religious allegiances are freer and the forms of expression of the religion are more varied in the adopted country, which does not have the constraints of tradition and prohibitions that exist in the countries of origin. The overt expression of the religion is not the same among all adherents of a particular religion. "More often, like any form of affirmative identity, individuals operate in a system of differentiations in direct competition with other possible constructions."

Social innovations constitute another area of research that could be particularly fruitful. Groups, associations, and organizations in minority communities and in the mainstream society can be quite creative in dealing with different issues of intergroup contacts and integration. It would seem that analyses of such "social experiments" – those that succeed and those that fail – would be significant sources of insights for theoretical and policy purposes.

Notes

INTRODUCTION

1 An interesting issue, though beyond the scope of this book, is why religion has taken a back seat in research on immigrant integration. This would be worthwhile examining. Some reasons may be the religious composition of the immigration flow, the impact of international events perceived as involving religious communities, the priorities of public-policy decision makers and their research funding agendas, or the prevailing attitudes among research professionals about the significance of religion in social life.

2 For a review of recent research on immigration and religion in the United States, see Cadge and Ecklund (2007).

3 For a review of the history of the various non-Christian religious minorities in Canada, see Bramadat and Seljak (2005).

4 For brief reviews of some dimensions of the cultural evolution of Canada see, for example, Cole (1971), Cook (1977), Levitt (1981), and Breton (1988).

5 For an analysis of the literature on these two approaches, see McKay (1982).

6 See Mol (1961: chap. 3) for an earlier discussion of churches and immigrants. Mol deals with the role that churches play in the adaptation of immigrants and the ways in which the church as institution and organization evolves under the influence of immigration.

CHAPTER ONE

1 Admittedly, there are other ways of classifying the issues that confront immigrants.
2 On the functions of religion for individuals, see Batson and Stocks (2004).
3 On the role of religion and religious organizations in the transplantation experience of immigrants, see also Mol (1961) and Menjivar (2003).
4 On the symbolic construction of community, see Cohen (1985).
5 On religious communities as a source of social capital, see Guest (2003), especially chapter 7.
6 This is discussed further in a later chapter.
7 For a similar pattern of difference between women and men, see Suh (2009). The findings of this research are discussed in chapter 4.
8 Two other styles identified are the deferring style, in which individuals "defer" problem solving to God, and the collaborative style, in which both the individual and God are understood to be active participants in the problem-solving process (Maynard et al. 2001, 66).

CHAPTER TWO

1 On the issue of threats and identity, see Ethier an Deaux (1994).
2 The survey of 1,002 randomly selected Canadians was conducted by Angus Reid Strategies in 2009 for *Maclean's* magazine. "The margin of error is +/- 3.1 percent, 19 times out of 20. The results were statistically weighted for education, age, gender and region to ensure a sample representative if the adult population of Canada" (Geddes 2009, 24).
3 The percentages with such perceptions of Hindu teachings, Judaism, and Buddhism are 13, 14, and 4 respectively.
4 The expression is from Goffman (1958).
5 See also Haddad (2009).
6 The changing role of churches and other religious organizations is discussed in chapter 4.
7 In the study of the relation between religion and inter-group attitudes, such as prejudice, it is important to distinguish between two

approaches: one that focuses on individual differences and one that focuses on the dynamics of inter-group relations (see Jackson and Hunsberger (1999) and Hunsberger and Jackson (2005).

8 For a review of the literature on the relation between religion and intergroup attitudes, see Hunsberger and Jackson (2005).

9 See chapter 5 for a more detailed description of this paradigm.

10 Suicide bombing is revealing in this regard. For analyses of the phenomenon, see Pape (2005), Brym and Araja (2008), and Brym (2008).

11 See chapter 5 for a more detailed description of this paradigm.

CHAPTER THREE

1 For discussions of the relationship between ethnicity and religion see, for example, Abramson (1980), Hammond and Warner (1993), and Kivisto (2007).

2 As an analytic category, ascription refers to those aspects of religious identity believed to be essential and unchangeable because of the circumstances of one's birth, whereas achievement, choice, practice, and performance refer to those things people do in order to create a sense of religious identity (Cadge and Davidman 2006, 24–5).

3 The conflict between Protestants and Catholics in Northern Ireland seems to be a case in point.

4 This has been noted in relation to Asian Buddhists in Toronto (McLellan 1999, 210).

CHAPTER FOUR

1 Gitelman (2009, 307–8) quotes Dobbelaere's view of secularization as meaning three things: "(1) functional differentiation in society, so that religion becomes one subsystem among others and loses its overarching claim; (2) organizational secularization, involves the change in values, beliefs, morals, and rituals of a religious group ... ; (3) individual secularization means the diminishing congruence between the norms of religious groups in beliefs, rituals, and morals and the attitudes and conduct of their members."

2 This expression is the title of a book on the rise and fall of the Catholic Church in Ireland, in which Inglis (1998) argues that the

Church's moral monopoly declined because it lost its control over sources of social capital.

3 See also Coser (1961) and Sieber (1974).

4 The Non-Official Languages Survey consisted of a sample of 2,433 respondents from three North European groups (German, Dutch, and Scandinavian), three East European groups (Ukrainian, Polish, and Hungarian), three South European groups (Italian, Greek, and Portuguese), and Chinese.

5 The index of ethnic-church affiliation was based on questions about the composition of the church with which they are associated and about the language used in conversations with priest, rabbi, or minister (Reitz 1980, 115).

6 The Longitudinal Survey of Immigrants to Canada conducted by Statistics Canada in early 2000.

7 The three time periods were 2001 (six months after migration), 2003, and 2005.

8 "Enquête sur l'établissement des nouveaux immigrants" carried out by the Quebec government during the 1990s.

9 This was the Ethnic Diversity Survey (EDS), conducted by Statistics Canada and the Department of Canadian Heritage in 2002. The target population was individuals aged fifteen years or over living in private households in the ten provinces. The survey was administered via a thirty-five- to forty-minute telephone interview conducted in nine languages: English, French, Cantonese, Mandarin, Italian, Portuguese, Punjabi, Spanish, and Vietnamese. The final EDS sample consisted of 41,666 respondents, representing a response rate of approximately 73 per cent. For more detailed information and analysis of the survey, see Reitz et al. (2009).

10 Religious services did not include special events such as weddings, funerals, baptisms, bar mitzvahs, and so on.

11 I am grateful to Mai Phan for carrying out this analysis.

12 On gender differences in images of God, see Nelsen et al. (1985).

13 In an inter-religious union, each partner is from a different religious group. For example a married couple consisting of a Buddhist and a Roman Catholic would be considered inter-religious. Unions of people from different Protestant denominations are not defined as inter-religious.

14 For another study of the process of individualization among Muslims in Europe, see Fadil (2005).

15 The survey included several items revealing the respondent's attitude concerning of diversity: an acceptance of people with different life styles; finding that being gay or lesbian is acceptable; disagreeing with views such as "that the ideal society is one in which people are sufficiently similar to feel at home with one another"; "that immigrants cannot expect to be considered as fully Canadian as those who were born and raised here"; "that ethnic, cultural and racial groups should try as much as possible to blend into Canadian society."

16 Five ethnic groups – English, German, Italian, Jewish, and Ukrainian – are included in this part of the study because there were enough cases to examine variations across generations.

17 The types of obligations considered were helping a group member find a job, marrying within the group, supporting group needs and causes, and having the children speak the ethnic language.

18 The religiosity index is based on (1) the existence or not of a religious affiliation, (2) religious attendance, (3) the frequency of religious activities, and (4) the importance attached to religion in one's life.

19 The percentages who are "highly religious" among immigrants from different regions of the world are as follows: Southern Asia, 65; South-East Asia, 56; Oceania, 55; Central America, South America, and the Caribbean, 52; Africa, 50; United States, 39; Southern Europe, 34; West Central Asia and the Middle East, 33; Eastern Europe, 27; Western and Northern Europe, 24, and East Asia, 21 (Clark and Schellenberg 2006, 8).

20 On this evolution, see Bayat (2010).

21 The section of the next chapter "Offering a paradigm through which the new society is defined" is relevant for the formulation of hypotheses in this connection.

CHAPTER FIVE

1 The communities studied were Catholic, Protestant, Muslim, Hindu, and Sikh.

CHAPTER SIX

1 The following sections draw heavily from Yang and Ebaugh (2001), Chafetz and Ebaugh (2002), and Haddad (1983).
2 There are congregations that are multi-ethnic simply because of the composition of the neighbourhoods in which they are located.
3 On the symbolic role of management in organizations, see, for example, Selznick (1957) and Pfeffer (1981).
4 For a discussion of political competition and structures in ethnic communities, see Breton (1991, chap. 2).

CHAPTER SEVEN

1 See below for a discussion of *eruv*.
2 Chapter 8 is devoted to a discussion of the institutional context and of its possible impact on the accommodation of minority religious communities.
3 See chap. 5.
4 See chap. 2.
5 See chap. 2 for a discussion of the attitudes and the perception of attitudes in the mainstream society.
6 An *eruv* is "Orthodox Jewry's physical demarcation of territory that its followers recognize as private space for purposes of Sabbath observance" (Siemiatycki 2005, 256). *Eruvin* is the plural of *eruv*.
7 Today *eruvim* exist in more than 200 cities around the world, including several Canadian cities (Siemiatycki 2005, 260).
8 For more information, see the Quebec Ministry of Education website.
9 About thirty Muslim women were honoured by the Canadian Council of Muslim Women for their social involvement within and beyond their own communities.

CHAPTER EIGHT

1 See also Kastoryano (2002).
2 "Pillarization" refers to the social and institutional coexistence of separate subcultural groups: Roman Catholic, orthodox Calvinist, and

secular. They are called "pillars" or "blocs" (Lijphart 1968, 16–17). Each has its political party, interest groups, communication media, educational institutions, and interpersonal networks (chapter 2).

3 Grim and Finke (2006) group these modalities under "government regulation" and "government favoritism." The first refers to the first three dimensions in Koenig's analysis and the second to the other three. Using a number of empirical indices, they assign a "score" to a large number of countries. A high score indicates a high degree of regulation or favouritism. For the countries discussed above, the scores for regulation and favouritism are as follows: France, 3.9 and 5.5; Germany, 2.2 and 4.7; Denmark, 0.8 and 6.7; The Netherlands, 0.0 and 3.0; Canada, 0.0 and 6.5; Sweden, 0.0 and 2.7; and the United Kingdom, 0.0 and 1.0. Of the 196 countries in the study, Saudi Arabia scores the highest.

4 Citizenship policies that place significant restrictions on the timing and conditions of naturalization can also have the effect of confining newcomers to their community and of discouraging integration in the larger society (Duyvené de Wit and Koopmans 2005, 54–7).

5 Religious groups that are not already established as mainstream groups.

6 The countries mentioned in parentheses are those discussed briefly elsewhere in this chapter.

7 On the matter of religion and Canadian identity, see also Murphy and Perrin (1996) and Mathews, 1988 (chapter 5: "Religion in Canada: Its Effect on Canadian Identity").

8 Grant (1977) notes that "if the churches have occupied themselves only fitfully with the quest for a Canadian *identity*, they have been deeply engaged from the beginning in an attempt to shape a Canadian *character*" (8, emphasis in original).

9 See also Moir (2002).

10 See also O'Toole (1985) and Lochhead (1991).

11 See also Lisée (2007), 10, 19–21.

12 Measures to accommodate the French language in Canada were considered by some to be a major threat to the identity and even survival of English and anglophones. Two of the manifestations of that reaction were the Association for the Protection of English in Canada and books such as *Bilingual Today, French Tomorrow* (Andrew 1977).

CONCLUSION

1 Some minority Christian groups have also found themselves in a
   similar situation. For example, Van Dijk (1998) found that ethnic
   persistence is higher among Dutch-Canadian Calvinists than among
   Dutch-Canadian Catholics and that Calvinists are also more likely to
   join churches and organizations that serve their ethnic group. The
   Calvinists' participation in ethnic churches may be due to the fact
   that there were no (or few) mainstream Calvinists religious institutions in which they could participate whereas Dutch-Canadian
   Catholics had access to many mainstream Catholic churches.
2 Some examples were noted in chapter 7.

References

Abramson, Harold J. 1980. "Religion," Pp. 869–75 in Stephan
  Thernstrom (ed.), *Harvard Encyclopedia of American Ethnic
  Groups*. Cambridge, MA: Harvard University Press.
Abu-Laban, Baha. 1983. "The Canadian Muslim Community:
  The Need for a New Survival Strategy." In Earle H. Waugh, Baha
  Abu-Laban, and Regula B. Qureshi (eds), *The Muslim Community
  in North America*. Edmonton: University of Alberta Press.
Ajrouch, Kristine. 1999. "Family and Ethnic Identity in an Arab-
  American Community." Pp. 129–39 in Michael W. Sieleiman (ed),
  Arabs in America: Building a New Future. Philadelphia: Temple
  University Press.
Ajrouch, Kristine, and Abdi M. Kusow. 2007. "Racial and religious
  contexts: Situational identities among Lebanese and Somali Muslim
  immigrants." *Ethnic and Racial Studies*, 30: 72–94.
Alba, Richard. 2005. "Bright vs. blurred Boundaries: Second-
  generation assimilation and exclusion in France, Germany, and the
  United States." *Ethnic and Racial Studies*, 28: 20–49.
Allievi, Stefano. 1999. "Pour une sociologie des conversions: lorsque des
  Européens deviennent musulmans." *Social Compass* 46: 283–300.
Amarasingam, Amarnath. 2008. "Religion and Ethnicity among Sri
  Lankan Tamil Youth in Ontario." *Canadian Ethnic Studies*, 40:
  149–69.
Andrew, J.V. 1977. *Bilingual Today, French Tomorrow*. Richmond Hill,
  ON: BMG.

Armstrong, Jane. 2009. "Building diversity: City pins big hopes on mosque." *The Globe and Mail*, June 10, A7.

Bader, Christopher, and Paul Froese. 2005. "Images of God: The Effect of Personal Theologies on Moral Attitudes, Political Affiliation, and Religious Behavior." *Interdisciplinary Journal of Research on Religion*, 1: 1–24.

Bader, Veit. 2007. "The Governance of Islam in Europe: The Perils of Modeling." *Journal of Ethnic and Migration Studies*, 33: 871–86.

– 2009. "The Governance of Religious Diversity: Theory, Research, and Practice." Pp. 43–72 in Paul Bramadat and Matthias Koenig (eds), *International Migration and the Governance of Religious Diversity*. Montreal: McGill-Queen's University Press.

Banerjee, Sikata, and Harold Coward. 2005. "Hindus in Canada: Negotiating Identity in a 'Different' Homeland." In Paul Bramadat and David Seljak (eds), *Religion and Ethnicity in Canada*. Toronto: Pearson Education Canada.

Bankston, Carl L. III, and Min Zhou. 1996. "The Ethnic Church, Ethnic Identification, and the Social Adjustment of Vietnamese Adolescents." *Review of Religious Studies*, 38: 18–35.

Barazangi, Nimat Hafez. 1989. "Arab Muslim identity transition: Parents and youth." Pp. 65–81 in Baha Abu-Laban and Michael W. Suleiman (eds), *Arab Americans: Continuity and Change*. Belmont, MA: Association of Arab-American University Graduates.

Barot, Rohit. 1993. "Religion, Ethnicity and Social Change: An Introduction." Pp. 1–16 in Rohit Barot (ed), *Religion and Ethnicity: Minorities and Social Change in the Metropolis*. Kampen, Netherlands: Kok Pharos.

Barth, Fredrik. 1969. *Ethnic Groups and Boundaries*. Boston: Little, Brown.

Bartlett, Jamie, Jonathan Birdwell, and Michael King. 2010. *The Edge of Violence: A Radical Approach to Extremism*. London: Demos.

Bastenier, Albert. 1998. "L'Incidence du facteur religieux dans la 'conscience ethnique' des immigrés marocains en Belgique." *Social Compass*, 45: 195–218.

Batson, C. Daniel, and E.L. Stocks. 2004. "Religion: Its Core Psychological Functions." In J. Greenberg, S.L. Koole, and T. Pyszczynski (eds), *Handbook of Experimental Existential Psychology*. New York: Guilford Press.

Bayat, Asef. 2010. *Life as Politics: How Ordinary People Change the Middle East*. Stanford, CA: Stanford University Press.

Berger, Peter. 1967. *The Sacred Canopy: Elements of a Sociological Theory of Religion*. Garden City, NY: Doubleday.

Berry, John W. 1990. 'Psychology of Acculturation: Understanding Individuals Moving between Cultures.' In R. Brislin (ed), *Applied Cross-Cultural Psychology*. Newbury Park, CA: Sage.

– J.S. Phinney, D.L. Sam, and P. Vedder. 2006. *Immigrant Youth in Cultural Transition: Acculturation, Identity and Adaptation across National Contexts*. Mahwah, NJ: Lawrence Erlbaum Associates.

Betz, Hans-Georg, and Carol Johnson. 2004. "Against the Current – Stemming the Tide: the Nostalgic Ideology of the Contemporary Radical Populist Right." *Journal of Political Ideologies*, 9: 311–27.

Beyer, Peter. 2005. "The Future of Non-Christian Religions in Canada: Patterns of Religious Identification among Recent Immigrants and their Second Generation, 1981–2001." *Studies in Religion*, 34: 165–96.

– 2008. "From Far and Wide: Canadian Religious and Cultural Diversity in Global/Local Context." In Lori O. Beaman and Peter Beyer (eds), *Religion and Diversity in Canada*. Leiden: Brill

Bibby, Reginald. 1987. *Fragmented Gods: The Poverty and Potential of Religion in Canada*. Toronto: Irving.

– 2004. *Restless Churches: The Renaissance of Religion in Canada*. Toronto: Novalis/St. Paul University.

Billings, Dwight B. 1990. "Religion as Opposition: A Gramscian Analysis." *American Journal of Sociology* 96: 1–31.

Blumer, Herbert. 1958. "Race Prejudice as a Sense of Group Position." *Pacific Sociological Review*, 1: 3–7.

Bobo, Lawrence, and Vincent L. Hutchings. 1996. "Perception of Racial Group Competition: Extending Blumer's Theory of Group Position to a Multiracial Social Context." *American Sociological Review*, 61: 951–72.

Boldt, Edward D. 1978. "Structural Tightness, Autonomy, and Observability: An Analysis of Hutterite Conformity and Orderliness." *Canadian Journal of Sociology*, 3: 349–63.

Boisvert, Mathieu. 2005. "Buddhists in Canada: Identity and Commitment." In Bramadat, Paul, and David Seljak (eds), *Religion and Ethnicity in Canada*. Toronto: Pearson Education Canada.

Bouchard, Gérard, and Charles Taylor. 2008. *Building the Future: A Time for Reconciliation.* Abridged Report (of the Consultation Commission on Accommodation Practices Related to Cultural Differences). Quebec City: Gouvernement du Québec.

Bramadat, Paul. 2005. "Beyond Christian Canada: Religion and Ethnicity in a Multicultural Society. In Paul Bramadat and David Seljak (eds), *Religion and Ethnicity in Canada.* Toronto: Pearson Education Canada.

– and David Seljak (eds). 2005. *Religion and Ethnicity in Canada.* Toronto: Pearson Education Canada.

Breton, Raymond. 1988. "From Ethnic to Civic Nationalism." *Ethnic and Racial Studies,* 11: 85–102.

– 1991. *The Governance of Ethnic Communities: Political Structures and Processes in Canada.* New York: Greenwood Press.

– 1992. "Collective Dimensions of the Cultural Transformation of Ethnic Communities and the Larger Society." In Jean Burnet (ed), *Migration and the Transformation of Cultures.* Toronto: Multicultural History Society of Ontario.

– Norbert J. Hartmann, Jos L. Lennards, and Paul Reed. 2004. *A Fragile Social Fabric? Fairness, Trust and Commitment in Canada.* Montreal: McGill-Queen's University Press.

Brown, David L., and Jane C. Brown. 1983. "Organizational Microcosms and Ideological Negotiation." In Max H. Bazerman (ed) *Negotiating in Organizations.* Thousand Oaks, CA: Sage.

Brym, Robert J. 2008. "Religion, politics, and suicide bombing: An interpretive essay," *Canadian Journal of Sociology,* 33: 89–108.

– and Bader Araj. 2008. "Palestinian suicide bombing revisited: A critique of the outbidding thesis." *Political Science Quarterly,* 123: 485–500.

Cadge, Wendy, and Lynn Davidman. 2006. "Ascription, Choice, and the construction of religious identities in the contemporary US." *Journal for the Scientific Study of Religion,* 45: 23–38.

– and Elaine Howard Ecklund. 2007. "Immigration and Religion." *Annual Review of Sociology,* 33: 359–79.

Cao, Nanlai. 2005. "The Church as a Surrogate Family for Working Class Immigrant Chinese Youth: An Ethnography of Segmented Assimilation." *Sociology of Religion,* 66: 183–200.

Cesari, Jocelyne. 2004a. *When Islam and Democracy Meet: Muslims in Europe and in the United States*. New York: Palgrave Macmillan.

– 2004b. "Les Enjeux de l'Institutionnalisation de l'Islam." In U. Manço (ed), *Reconnaissance et discrimination: la présence de l'islam en occident*.

Chafetz, Janet S., and Helen R. Ebaugh. 2002. "Lessons from American Immigrant Congregations." In Ebaugh and Chafetz (eds), *Religion across Borders: Transnational Immigrant Networks*. New York: Altamira Press.

Chen, Carolyn. 2002. "The Religious Varieties of Ethnic Presence: A Comparison between a Taiwanese Immigrant Buddhist Temple and an Evangelical Christian Church." *Sociology of Religion*, 63: 215–38.

– 2006. "From Filial Piety to Religious Piety: Evangelical Christianity Reconstructing Taiwanese Immigrant Families in the United States." *International Migration Review*, 40: 573–602.

Chong, Kelly H. 1998. "What It Means to Be Christian: The Role of Religion in the Construction of Ethnic Identity and Boundary among Second-Generation Korean Americans." *Sociology of Religion*, 59: 259–86. *Christian Century*. 2002. "Poll: Americans Shun Conversion Goals." May 8– 15, 16.

Clarke, Peter. 1998. "Islamic Fundamentalism and the Construction of the Self in Post-Modern Society." In Joorgen S. Nielsen (ed), *The Christian-Muslim Frontier: Chaos, Clash or Dialogue*. London: I.B. Tauris.

Clark, Warren. 2006. "Interreligious Unions in Canada." *Canadian Social Trends*, No. 82: 17–21.

Clark, Warren, and Grant Schellenberg. 2006. "Who Is Religious?" *Canadian Social Trends*, No. 81: 2–9.

Cohen, Anthony P. 1985. *The Symbolic Construction of Community*. London: Tavistock.

Cole, Douglas. 1971. "The problem of 'nationalism' and 'imperialism' in British settlement colonies." *Journal of British Studies*, 10: 160–82.

Coleman, James S. 1970. "Social Inventions." *Social Forces*, 49: 163–73.

– "Social Capital and the Creation of Human Capital." *American Journal of Sociology*, 94 Supplement: S95–S120.

- 1990. *Foundations of Social Theory*. Cambridge, MA: Belknap Press of Harvard University Press.

Connor, Philip. 2008. "Increase or Decrease? The Impact of the International Migratory Event on Immigrant Religious participation." *Journal for the Scientific Study of Religion*, 47: 243–57.

- 2009. "Immigrant Religiosity in Canada: Multiple Trajectories." *Journal of International Migration and Integration*, 10: 159–75.

Cook, Ramsay. 1977. *The Maple Leaf Forever: Essays on Nationalism and Politics in Canada*. Toronto: Macmillan of Canada.

Coser, Rose Laub. 1961. "Insulation from Observability and Types of Social Conformity." *American Sociological Review*, 26: 28–39.

Coward, Harold. 2000. "Hinduism in Canada." In Harold Coward, John R. Hinnells, and Raymond Brady Williams (eds), *The South Asian Religious Diaspora in Britain, Canada, and the United States*. Albany, NY: State University of New York.

Coward, Harold, and Heather Botting. 1999. "The Hindu Diaspora in Western Canada." In T.S. Rukmani (ed), *Hindu Diaspora: Global Perspectives*. Montreal: Chair of Hindu Studies, Department of Religion, Concordia University.

Coward, Harold, and Leslie Kawamura (eds). 1977. *Religion and Ethnicity*. Waterloo, ON: Wilfrid Laurier University Press.

Davie, Grace. 1993. "Believing without Belonging: A Framework for Religious Transmission." *Recherches Sociologiques* (3): 17–37.

Daynes, Sarah. 1999. "Processus de conversions et modes d'identification à l'islam: l'exemple de la France er des États-Unis." *Social Compass* 46: 313–23.

Deshen, Shlomo. 1974. "Political Ethnicity and Cultural Ethnicity in Israel during the 1960s." In Anbner Cohen (ed), *Urban Ethnicity*. London: Tavistock.

Doomernik, Jeroen. 1995. "The Institutionalization of Turkish Islam in Germany and The Netherlands: A Comparison." *Ethnic and Racial Studies*, 18: 46–63.

Driedger, Leo. 1980. "Nomos-Building on the Prairies: Construction of Indian, Hutterite, and Jewish Sacred Canopies." *Canadian Journal of Sociology*, 5: 341–56.

Duyvené de Wit, Thom, and Ruud Koopmans. 2005. "The Integration of Ethnic Minorities into Political Culture: The Netherlands, Germany and Great Britain." *Acta Politica*, 40: 50–73.

Eck, Diana L. 2001. *A New Religious America*. San Francisco: Harper.

Ecklund, Elaine Howard. 2005. "Models of Civic Responsibility: Korean Americans in Congregations with Different Ethnic Compositions." *Journal for the Scientific Study of Religion*, 44: 15–28.

Eid, Paul. 2003. "The Interplay between Ethnicity, Religion, and Gender among Second-Generation Christian and Muslim Arabs in Montreal." *Canadian Ethnic Studies*, 35: 30–55.

– 2007. *Being Arab. Ethnic and Religious Identity Building Among Second Generation Youth in Montreal*. Montreal: McGill-Queen's University Press.

Elias, Norbert, and John L. Scotson. 1994. *The Established and the Outsiders* (2nd ed). London: Sage.

Ethier, Kathleen A., and Kay Deaux. 1994. "Negotiating Social Identity When Contexts Change: Maintaining Identification and Responding to Threat." *Journal of Personality and Social Psychology*, 67: 243–51.

Fadil, Nadia. 2005. Individualizing Faith, Individualizing Identity: Islam and Young Muslim Women in Belgium." Pp. 85–97 in Jocelyne Cesari and Sean McLoughlin (eds), *European Muslims and the Secular State*. Aldershot, UK: Ashgate.

Fishman, Joshua. 1985. *The Rise and Fall of Ethnic Revival: Perspectives on Language and Ethnicity*. New York: Mouton.

Foley, Michael W., and Dean R. Hoge. 2007. *Religion and the New Immigrants: How Faith Communities Form Our Newest Citizens*. New York: Oxford University Press.

Foner, Nancy, and Richard Alba. 2008. "Immigrant Religion in the US and Western Europe: Bridge or Barrier to Inclusion?" *International Migration Review*, 42: 360–92.

Form, William. 2000. "Italian Protestants: Religion, Ethnicity, and Assimilation." *Journal for the Scientific Study of Religion*, 39: 307–20.

Gans, Herbert. 1979. "Symbolic Ethnicity: The Future of Ethnic Groups and Cultures." *Ethnic and Racial Studies*, 2: 1–20.

– 1994. "Symbolic Ethnicity and Symbolic Religiosity: Towards a Comparison of Ethnic and Religious Acculturation." *Ethnic and Racial Studies*, 17: 577–92.

Germain, Annick. 2004. "L'Aménagement des lieux de culte des minorités ethniques à Montréal: l'Autre, là où on ne l'attendais pas." In Anne Gotman (ed), *Villes et Hospitalité*. Paris: Éditions de la Maison des Sciences de l'Homme.

Geddes, John. 2009. "What Canadians Think of Sikhs, Jews, Christians, Muslims." *Maclean's*, May 4, 20–4.

Gitelman, Zvi. (ed.). 2009. *Religion or Ethnicity? Jewish Identities in Evolution*. New Brunswick, NJ: Rutgers University Press.

Goffman, Irving. 1958. *The Presentation of Self in Everyday Life*. Garden City, NY: Doubleday.

Goldscheider, Calvin. 2009a. "Judaism, Community and Jewish Culture in American Life." In Zvi Gitelman (ed), *Religion or Ethnicity? Jewish Identities in Evolution*. New Brunswick, NJ: Rutgers University Press.

Goldscheider, Calvin. 2009b. "Immigration and the Transformation of American Jews: Assimilation, Distinctiveness, and Community." In Richard Alba et al. (eds), *Immigration and Religion in America*. New York: New York University Press.

Gordon, Daphne. 2007. "'We're Canadian and We're Muslim'" *Toronto Star*, October 26.

Grant, John W. 1977. "Religion and the Quest for a National Identity." In Peter Slater (ed), *Religion and Culture in Canada*. Toronto: Canadian Corporation for Studies in Religion.

Gray, John. 2008. "Faith in Reason: Secular Fantasies in a Godless Age." *Harper's Magazine*, January, 85–9.

Grim, Brian J., and Roger Finke. 2006. "International Religion Indexes: Government Regulation, Government Favoritism, and Social Regulation of Religion." *Interdisciplinary Journal of Research on Religion*, 2: 1–40.

Gross, Michael L. 1993. "Paradigms of Jewish Ethnicity: Methodological and Normative Implications." *Jewish Journal of Sociology*, 35: 34.

Guest, Kenneth J. 2003. *God in Chinatown: Religion and Survival in New York's Evolving Immigrant Community*. New York: New York University Press.

Haddad, Yvonne. 1983. "Arab Muslims and Islamic Institutions in America: Adaptation and Reform." In Sameer Y. Abraham and Nabel Abraham (eds), *Arabs in the New World*. Detroit, MI.: Wayne State University Press.

Haddad, Yvonne Yazbeck. 1994. "Maintaining the Faith of the Fathers: Dilemmas of Religious Identity in the Christian and

Muslim Arab-American Communities." Pp. 61–84 in Ernest McCarus (ed.), *The Development of Arab-American identity*. Ann Arbor, MI: University of Michigan Press.

– 2007. "The Post-9/11 *Hijab* as Ion." *Sociology of Religion*, 68: 253–67.

– 2009. "The Shaping of Arab and Muslim Identity in the United States." In Richard Alba et al. (eds), *Immigration and Religion in America*. New York: New York University Press.

Hagan, Jacqueline, and Helen Rose Ebaugh. 2003. "Calling upon the Sacred: Migrant's Use of Religion in the Migration Process." *International Migration Review*, 37: 1145–62.

Hall, Brian. 2006. "Social and Cultural Contexts in Conversion to Christianity Among Chinese American College Students." *Sociology of Religion*, 67: 131–47.

Hammond, Phillip E. 1992. *Religion and Personal Autonomy: The Third Disestablishment in America*. Columbia, SC: University of North Carolina Press.

Hammond, Phillip E., and Kee Warner. 1993. "Religion and Ethnicity in Late-Twentieth-Century America." *The Annals of the American Academy of Political and Social Sciences*, 527: 55–66.

Helly, Denise. 2004. "Are Muslims Discriminated against in Canada since September 2001?" *Canadian Ethnic Studies*, 6: 24–47.

Herberg, Will. 1960. *Protestant – Catholic – Jew*. Rev. edn. Garden City, NY.: Anchor Books.

Hewitt, John P. 1989. *Dilemmas of the American Self*. Philadelphia: Temple University Press.

Hirschman, Charles. 2004. "The Role of Religion in the Origins and Adaptation of Immigrant Groups in the US." *International Migration Review*, 38: 206–1233.

Hjarno, Jan. 1997. "Muslims in Denmark." In Gerd Nonneman et al. (eds), *Muslims in the New Europe*. UK: Ithaca Press.

Howard, Marc Morjé. 2009. *The Politics of Citizenship in Europe*. New York: Cambridge University Press.

Hunsberger, Bruce, and Lynne M. Jackson. 2005. "Religion, Meaning, and Prejudice." *Journal of Social Issues*, 61: 807–26.

Hurh, Won Moo, and Kwang Chung Kim. 1990. "Religious Participation of Korean Immigrants in the United States." *Journal for the Scientific Study of Religion*, 29: 19–43.

Inglis, Tom. 1998. *Moral Monopoly: The Rise and Fall of the Catholic Church in Modern Ireland* (2nd ed). Dublin: University College Press.

Introvigne, Massimo. 2005. "Niches in the Islamic Religious Market and Fundamentalism: Examples from Turkey and Other Countries." *Interdisciplinary Journal of Research on Religion*, 1: 2–25.

Isajiw, Wsevolod W. 1990. "Ethnic-Identity Retention." In Raymond Breton et al., *Ethnic Identity and Equality: Varieties of Experience in a Canadian City*. Toronto: University of Toronto Press.

Isin, Engin F., and Myer Siemiatycki. 2002. "Making Space for Mosques: Struggles for Urban Citizenship in Diasporic Toronto." In Sherene H. Razack (ed), *Race, Space and the Law*. Toronto: Between the Lines.

Jackson, Lynne M., and Bruce Hunsberger. 1999. "An Intergroup Perspective of Religion and Prejudice." *Journal for the Scientific Study of Religion*, 38: 509–23.

Jacobsen, Christine. 2005. "The Quest for Authenticity: Islamization among Muslim Youth in Norway." In Jocelyne Cesari and Sean McLoughlin (eds), *European Muslims and the Secular State*. Aldershot, UK: Ashgate.

Jacobson, Jessica. 1997. "Religion and Ethnicity: Dual and Alternative Sources of Identity among Young British Pakistanis." *Ethnic and Racial Studies*, 20: 238–56.

James, W.C. 2006. "The Challenges of Religious Pluralism in Kingston, Ontario." *Canadian Journal of Urban Research*, 15 (Supplement): 50–66.

Jedwab, Jack. 2001. "Leadership, Governance, and the Politics of Identity in Canada." *Canadian Ethnic Studies*, 33: 4–38.

Kahani-Hopkins, Vered, and Nick Hopkins. 2002. "'Representing' British Muslims: The Strategic Dimension to Identity Construction." *Ethnic and Racial Studies*, 25: 288–309.

Kalilombe, Patrick. 1997. "Black Christianity in Britain." *Ethnic and Racial Studies*, 20: 306–24.

Kapsis, Robert E. 1978. "Black Ghetto Diversity and Anomie: A Sociopolitical View." *American Journal of Sociology*, 83: 1132–53.

Karakasoglu, Yasemin, and Gerd Nonneman. 1997. "Muslims in Germany, with Special Reference to the Turkish-Islamic Community."

Chap. 12 in Nonneman et al. (eds), *Muslim Communities in the New Europe*.

Kastoryano, Riva. 2002. *Negotiating Identities: States and Immigrants in France and Germany*. Princeton, NJ: Princeton University Press.

– 2004. "Religion and Incorporation: Islam in France and Germany." *International Migration Review*, 38: 1234–55.

Kepel, Gilles. 1997. "Islamic Groups in Europe: Between Community Affirmation and Social Crisis." In Steven Vertovec and Ceri Peach (eds), *Islam in Europe: The Politics of Religion and Community*. London: Macmillan.

Kettani, Houssain. 2010. "2010 World Muslim Population." *Proceedings of the 8th Hawaii International Conference on Arts and Humanities*, Honolulu, Hawaii.

Keung, Nicholas. 2008. "Twinning Builds bond between Muslims, Jews." *Toronto Star*, November 24.

Khosrokhavar, Farhad. 1997. *L'islam des jeunes*. Paris: Flammarion.

Kim, Illsoo. 1981. *New Urban Immigrants: The Korean Community in New York*. Princeton, NJ: Princeton University Press.

Kivisto, Peter. 2007. "Rethinking the Relationship between Ethnicity and Religion," In James A. Beckford and N.J. Demerath III (eds), *The Sage Handbook of the Sociology of Religion*. Los Angeles, CA: Sage.

Kivisto, Peter, and Ben Nefzger. 1993. "Symbolic Ethnicity and American Jews: The Relationship of Ethnic Identity to Behavior and Group Affiliation." *Social Science Journal*, 30: 1–12.

Knowles, Norman. 1995. "Religious Affiliation, Demographic Change and Family Formation among British Columbia's Chinese and Japanese Communities: A Case Study of Church of England Missions, 1861–1942." *Canadian Ethnic Studies*, 27: 59–80.

Koenig, Matthias. 2005a. "Introduction." *Canadian Diversity*, 4 (3): 3–6.

– 2005b. "Incorporating Muslim Migrants in Western Nation States: A Comparison of the United Kingdom, France and Germany." *Journal of International Migration and Integration*." 6: 219–34.

– 2007. "Europeanizing the Governance of Religious Diversity: An Institutionalist Account of Muslim Struggles for Public Recognition." *Journal of Ethnic and Migration Studies*, 33: 911–32.

– 2009. "How Nation-States Respond to Religious Diversity." In Paul
   Bramadat and Matthias Koenig (eds), *International Migration and
   the Governance of Religious Diversity*. Montreal: McGill-Queen's
   University Press.

Kucukcan, Talip. 1998. "Continuity and Change: Young Turks in
   London." In Steven Vertovec and Alisdair Rogers (eds), *Muslim
   European Youth: Reproducing Ethnicity, Religion, Culture*.
   Aldershot, UK: Ashgate.

Kurien, Prema A. 1998. "Becoming American by Becoming Hindu:
   Indian Americans Take their Place at the Multicultural Table." In
   Stephen Warner and Judith G. Wittner (eds), *Gathering in Diaspora:
   Religious Communities and the New Immigration*. Philadelphia:
   Temple University Press.

Lai, David Chuenyan, Jordan Paper, and Li Chuang Paper. 2005. In
   Paul Bramadat and David Seljak (eds), *Religion and Ethnicity in
   Canada*. Toronto: Pearson Education Canada.

Laidlaw, Stuart. 2007. "Sixteen Congregations Converge on Three
   Churches Each Sunday on a Corner That Has Come to Reflect the
   Changing Face of Toronto." *Toronto Star*, December 15.

– 2008. "Consecrated Ground Was Essential for the First Jews Who
   Came to Toronto and Stayed." *Toronto Star*, April 19.

Leveau, R. 1991. "Islam in France." Pp. 122–33 in W.A.R. Shadid and
   P.S. van Koningsveld (eds), *The Integration of Islam and Hinduism
   in Western Europe*. Kampen, Netherlands: Kok Pharos.

Levitt, Joseph. 1981. "Race and Nation in Canadian Anglophone
   Historiography." *Canadian Review of Studies in Nationalism*, 8:
   1–16.

Lewins, Frank W. 1978. "Religion and Ethnic Identity," In Hans Mol
   (ed), *Identity and Religion: International, Cross-Cultural
   Approaches*. London: Sage.

Lin, Ann Chih. 2009. "Muslim, Arab, and American: The Adaptation
   of Muslim Arab Immigrants to American society." In Richard Alba
   et al. (eds), *Immigration and Religion in America*. New York: New
   York University Press.

Lijphart, Arend. 1968. *The Politics of Accommodation: Pluralism and
   Democracy in The Netherlands*. Berkeley: University of California
   Press.

Lisée, Jean-François. 2007. *Nous*. Montreal: Boréal.

Lochhead, David. 1991. "The United Church of Canada and the Conscience of the Nation." In Robert E. VanderVerinen (ed), *Church and Canadian Culture*. New York: University Press of America.

Loewen, Royden. 2008. "The Poetics of Peoplehood: Ethnicity and Religion among Canada's Mennonites." In Paul Bramadat and David Seljak (eds), *Christianity and Ethnicity in Canada*. Toronto: University of Toronto Press.

Lyman, Stanford M., and William A. Douglass. 1973. "Ethnicity: Strategies of Collective and Individual Impression Management." *Social Research*, 40: 344–65.

Macey, Marie. 1999. "Class, Gender and Religious Influences on Changing Patterns of Pakistani Muslim Male Violence in Bradford." *Ethnic and Racial Studies*, 22: 845–66.

Mathews, Robin. 1988. *Canadian Identity: Major Forces Shaping the Life of a People*. Ottawa: Steel Rail.

Mattson, Ingrid. 2003. "How Muslims Use Islamic Paradigms to Define America." Pp. 199–215 in Yvonne Y. et al., *Religion and Immigration*. New York: Altamira Press.

Maynard, Elizabeth A., Richard L. Gorsuch, and Jeffrey P. Bjorck. 2001. "Religious Coping Style, Concept of God, and Personal Religious Variables in Threat, Loss, and Challenge Situations." *Journal for the Scientific Study of Religion*, 14: 65–74.

McAndrew, Marie, Bechir Oueslati, and Denise Healy. 2007. "L'évolution de traitement de l'islam et des cultures musulmanes dans les manuels scolaires québécois de langue française du secondaire." *Canadian Ethnic Studies / Études Ethniques au Canada* 39: 173–88.

McDonough, Sheila, and Hoam Hoodfar. 2005. "Muslims in Canada: From Ethnic Groups to Religious Community." In Paul Bramadat and David Seljak (eds), *Religion and Ethnicity in Canada*. Toronto: Pearson Education Canada.

McGown, Rima Berns. 1999. *Muslims in the Diaspora: The Somali Communities of London and Toronto*. Toronto: University of Toronto Press.

McKay, James. 1982. "An Exploratory Synthesis of Primordial and Mobilizationist Approaches to Ethnic Phenomena." *Ethnic and Racial Studies*, 54: 395–420.

McLellan, Janet. 1999. *Many Petals of the Lotus: Five Asian Buddhist Communities in Toronto*. Toronto: University of Toronto Press.

– 2004. "Cambodian Refugees in Ontario: Religious Identities, Social Cohesion and Transnational Linkages." *Canadian Ethnic Studies*, 36: 101–18.

Menjivar, Cecilia. 2003. "Religion and Immigration in Comparative Perspective: Catholic and Evangelical Salvadorans in San Francisco, Washington, DC, and Phoenix." *Sociology of Religion*, 64: 21–45.

Milot, Micheline. 2009. "Modus Co-Vivendi: Religious Diversity in Canada." Pp. 105–29 in Paul Bramadat and Matthias Koenig (eds), *International Migration and the Governance of Religious Diversity*. Montreal: McGill-Queen's University Press.

Min, Pyong Gap. 1992. "The Structure and Social Functions of Korean Immigrant Churches in the US." *International Migration Review*, 26: 1370–94.

– 2005. "Religion and the Maintenance of Ethnicity among Immigrants: A Comparison of Indian Hindus and Korean Protestants." In Karen I. Leonard et al. (eds), *Immigrant Faiths: Transforming Religious Life in America*. New York: Altamira Press.

Minkenberg, Michael. 2008. "Religious Legacies and the Politics of Multiculturalism.' In Ariane Chebel d'Appollonia and Simon Reich (eds), *Immigration, Integration and Security: America, Europe in Comparative Perspective*. Pittsburgh: University of Pittsburgh Press.

Moaddel, Mansoor. 2005. *Islamic Modernism, Nationalism and Fundamentalism*. Chicago: University of Chicago Press.

Mobasher, Mohsen. 2006. "Cultural Trauma and Ethnic Identity Formation among Iranian Immigrants in the United States." *American Behavioral Scientist*, 50: 100–17.

Moir, John S. 2002. "The Search for a Christian Canada." Chap. 2 in John S. Moir, *Christianity in Canada: Historical Essays*. Gravelbourg, SK: Laverdure and Associates.

Mol, J.J. 1961. *Churches and Immigrants*. The Hague: Research Group for European Migration Problems.

Mossman, Matt. 2011. "Mosque Makeovers: Reimagining a Sacred Space." *Walrus*, 8 (April), 62–5.

Mullins, Mark R. 1987. "The Life-Cycle of Ethnic Churches in Sociological Perspective." *Japanese Journal of Religious Studies*, 14: 321–34.

- 1988. "The Organizational Dilemmas of Ethnic Churches: A Case Study of Japanese Buddhism in Canada." *Sociological Analysis,* 49: 217–33.

- 1989. *Religious Minorities in Canada: A Sociological Study of the Japanese Experience.* Lewiston, NY: Edwin Mellen Press.

Murphy, Terrence, and Roberto Perrin. 1996. *A Concise History of Christianity in Canada.* Toronto: Oxford University Press.

Nagata, Judith. 1987. "The Role of Christian Churches in the Integration of Southeast Asian Immigrants in Toronto." *Contributions to Southeast Asian Ethnography,* No. 6: 39–59.

Naguib, Saphina-Amal. 2002. "The Northern Way: Muslim Communities in Norway." Pp. 161–74 in Yvonne Y. Haddad and Jane J. Smith (eds), *Muslim Minorities in the West.* Oxford: Altamira Press.

Nayar, Kamala E. 2004. "Religion among the Three Generations." In *The Sikh Diaspora in Vancouver. Three Generations Amid Tradition, Modernity, and Multiculturalism.* Toronto: University of Toronto Press.

Nelsen, Hart M., Neil H. Cheek, Jr., and Paul Au. 1985. "Gender Differences in Images of God." *Journal for the Scientific Study of Religion,* 24: 396–402.

Nielsen, J.S. 1991. "Muslim Organizations in Europe." In W.A.R. Shadid and P.S. van Koningsveld (eds), *The Integration of Islam and Hinduism in Western Europe.* Kampen, Netherlands: Kok Pharos.

Obadia, Lionel. 2000. "Une tradition au delà de la modernité : l'institutionnalisation de bouddhisme tibétain en France." *Recherches Sociologiques,* 31: 76–88.

O'Connell, Joseph T. 2000. "Sikh Religio-Ethnic Experience in Canada." In Harold Coward, John R. Hinnells, and Raymond Brady Williams (eds), *The South Asian Religious Diaspora in Britain, Canada, and the United States.* Albany: State University of New York.

O'Toole, Roger. 1985. "Society, the Sacred and the Secular: Sociological Observations on the Changing Role of Religion in Canadian Culture." *Canadian Issues/ Thèmes Canadiens,* 7: 99–117.

Pape, Robert A. 2005. *Dying to Win: The Strategic Logic of Suicide Terrorism.* New York: Random House.

Peach, Ceri. 2004. "Reconnaissance de l'islam, mais marginalité sociale des musulmans." Pp. 169–89 in U. Manço (ed), *Reconnaissance et discrimination : la présence de l'islam en occident.* Paris: L'Harmattan.

Pfeffer, Jeffrey. 1981. *Power in organizations*. Boston: Pitman.

Phan, Mai, and Raymond Breton. 2009. "Inequalities and Patterns of Social Attachments in Quebec and the Rest of Canada." In Jeffrey G. Reitz, Raymond Breton, Karen Kisiel Dion, and Kenneth L. Dion, *Multiculturalism and Social Cohesion: Potentials and Challenges of Diversity*. N.p.: Springer.

Portes, Alejandro, and Julia Sensenbrenner. 1993. "Embeddedness and Immigration: Notes on the Social Determinants of Economic Action." *American Journal of Sociology*, 98: 1320–50.

Putnam, Robert D. 1993. "The Prosperous Community: Social Capital and Public Life." *The American Prospect*, 4, no. 13: 35–42.

Ramji, Rubina. 2008. "Creating a Genuine Islam: Second Generation Muslims Growing Up in Canada." *Canadian Diversity/Diversité canadienne*, 6 (2): 104–09.

Rath, Jan, Rinus Penninx, Kees Groenendijk, and Asrid Meyer 2001. *Western Europe and its Islam*. Leiden: Brill.

Read, Jen'nan Ghazal. 2003. "The Sources of Gender Role Attitudes among Christian and Muslim Arab-American Women." *Sociology of Religion*, 64: 207–22.

Redekop, Benjamin W. 1992. "Germanism among Mennonite Brethren Immigrants in Canada, 1930–1960." *Canadian Ethnic Studies*, 24: 26–42.

Reitz, Jeffrey G. 1980. *The Survival of Ethnic Groups*. Toronto: McGraw-Hill.

– and Raymond Breton. 1994. *The Illusion of Difference: Realities of Ethnicity in Canada and the United States*. Toronto: C.D. Howe Institute.

– Rupa Banerjee, Mai Phan, and Jordan Thompson. 2009. "Race, Religion and the Social Integration of New Immigrant Minorities in Canada." *International Migration Review*, 43: 695–726.

– Raymond Breton, Karen Kisiel Dion, and Kenneth L. Dion: 2009. *Multiculturalism and Social Cohesion: Potentials and Challenges of Diversity*. N.p.: Springer.

Roof, Wade Clark. 1993. *A Generation of Seekers*. San Francisco: Harper.

– 2003. "Religion and Spirituality: Toward an Integrated Analysis." In Michelle Dillon (ed). *Handbook of the Sociology of Religion*. New York: Cambridge University Press.

Rousseau, Louis. 2005. "La construction religieuse de la nation." *Recherches Sociographiques*, 46: 437–52.

Roy, Olivier. 1992. "L'islam en France : religion, communauté ethnique ou ghetto social?" In Bernard Lewis and Dominique Schnapper, *Musulmans en Europe*. Arles: Actes Sud.

– 2004. *Globalized Islam: The Search for a New Ummah*. New York: Columbia University Press.

Rumbaut, Rubén G. 2008. "Reaping What You Sew: Immigration and Reactive Ethnicity." *Applied Developmental Science* 12: 108–11.

Rutledge, Paul. 1991. Strategies for Ethnicity in Religion: The Employment of Religious Perceptions by Vietnamese People in Oklahoma City." *Asian Journal of Theology* 5: 176–85.

Rydgren, Jens. 2007. "The Sociology of the Radical Right." *Annual Review of Sociology*, 33: 241–62.

Salzman, Michael B., and Michael J. Halloran. 2004. "Cultural Trauma and Recovery." Chap. 15 in Jeff Greenberg, Sander L. Koole, and Tom Pyszczynski (eds), *Handbook of Experimental and Existential Psychology*. New York: Guilford Press.

Sander, Ake. 1991. "The Road from Musalla to Mosque: The Process of Integration and Institutionalization of Islam in Sweden." In W.A.R. Shadid and P.S. van Koningsveld (eds), *The Integration of Islam and Hinduism in Western Europe*. Kampen, Netherlands: Kok Pharos.

Sarna, Jonathan D. 1978. "From Immigrants to Ethnics: Toward a New Theory of 'Ethnicization'" *Ethnicity*, 5: 370–8.

Saunders, Doug. 2007. "An Iranian Sage Advises: Wait Out the 'Explosion ... of Fantasies.'" *The Globe and Mail*, March 24: F3.

Schiffauer, Werner. 2007. "From Exile to Diaspora: The Development of Transnational Islam in Europe." In Aziz Al-Azmeh and Effie Fokes (eds), *Islam in Europe: Diversity, Identity and Influence*. New York: Cambridge University Press.

Selznick, Philip. 1957. *Leadership in Administration*. New York: Harper and Row.

Shadid, W.A., and P.S. van Koningsveld. 1991. "Integration and Change." In W.A.R. Shadid and P.S. van Koningsveld (eds), *The Integration of Islam and Hinduism in Western Europe*. Kampen, Netherlands: Kok Pharos.

Shaheen, Jack G. 2003. "Reel Bad Arabs: How Hollywood Vilifies a People." *Annals of the American Academy of Political and Social Science*, 588: 171–93.

Sieber, Sam D. 1974. "Toward a Theory of Role Accumulation." *American Sociological Review*, 39: 567–78.

Siemiatycki, Myer. 2005. "Contesting Sacred Urban Space: The Case of the *Eruv*." *Journal of International Migration and Integration*, 6: 255–70.

Smith, Timothy L.1971. "Lay Initiative in the Religious Life of American Immigrants, 1880–1950. In Tamara K. Hareven (ed), *Anonymous Americans: Explorations in 19th Century Social History.* Englewood Cliffs, NJ: Prentice-Hall.

– 1978. "Religion and Ethnicity in America." *American Historical Review*, 83: 1155–85.

Soper, J. Christopher, and Joel S. Fetzer. 2007. "Religious Institutions, Church-State History and Muslim Mobilisation in Britain, France and Germany." *Journal of Ethnic and Migration Studies*, 33: 933–44.

Sorenson, John. 1991. "Politics of Social Identity: Ethiopians in Canada". *Journal of Ethnic Studies,* 19: 67–87.

Stark, Rodney. 1972) "The Economics of Piety: Religious Commitment and Social Class." In Gerald W. Thielbar and Saul D. Feldman (eds), *Issues in Social Inequality.* Boston: Little, Brown.

Stark, Rodney, and William Bainbridge. 1985. *The Future of Religion. Secularization, Revival and Cult Formation.* Berkeley: University of California Press.

Stark, Rodney, and Roger Finke. 2000. *Acts of Faith: Explaining the Human Side of Religion.* Berkeley: University of California Press.

Statistics Canada. 2001. "Selected Religions" (20% sample). *Census of Population, 2001.* Ottawa: Statistics Canada.

Stevens, Gonneke W.J.M., Trees V.M. Pels, Wilma M. Vollebergh, and Alfons M. Crijnen. 2004. "Patterns of Psychological Acculturation in Adult and Adolescent Moroccan Immigrants Living in the Netherlands." *Journal of Cross-Cultural Psychology,* 35: 689–704.

Suh, Sharon A. 2009) "Buddhism, Rhetoric, and the Korean American Community." In Richard Alba, Albert J. Raboteau, and Josh DeWind (eds), *Immigration and Religion in America.* New York: New York University Press.

Sunier, Thijl. 2005. "Interests, Identities, and the Public Sphere: Representing Islam in the Netherlands since the 1980s." In Jocelyne Cesari and Sean McLoughlin (eds), *European Muslims and the Secular State*. Aldershot, UK: Ashgate.

Suttles, Gerald D. 1972. *The Social Construction of Communities.*" Chicago: University of Chicago Press.

Sutton, Philip W., and Stephen Vertigans. 2005. *Resurgent Islam: A Sociological Approach*. Cambridge, UK: Polity.

Swidler, Ann. 1986. "Culture in Action: Symbols and Strategies." *American Sociological Review*, 51: 273–86.

Szajkowski, Bogdan, Tim Niblock, and Gerd Nonneman. 1997. "Islam and Ethnicity in Eastern Europe: Concepts, Statistics, and a Note on the Polish Case." In Gerd Nonneman, Tim Niblock, and Bogdan Szajkowski (eds), *Muslim Communities in the New Europe*. Reading, UK: Ithaca Press.

Taylor, Charles. 1992. *Multiculturalism and "The Politics of Recognition."* Princeton, NJ: Princeton University Press.

Timmerman, Christiane. 2000. "Muslim Women and Nationalism: The Power of the Image." *Current Sociology*, 48: 15–27.

Valpy, Michael, and Joe Friesen. 2010. "A Twist of Faith." *Globe and Mail*, December 11, A16–A17.

Van der Lans, Jan, and Margo Rooijackers 1994. "Attitudes of Second Generation Turkish Immigrants towards Collective Religious Representations of Their Parental Culture." In Jozef Corveleyn and Dirk Hutsabaut (eds), *Belief and Unbelief: Psychological Perspectives*. Amsterdam: Rodopi.

Van Dijk, Joanne. 1998. "Ethnic Persistence among Dutch-Canadian Catholics and Calvinists." *Canadian Ethnic Studies*, 30: 23–49.

Vertovec, Steven. 1990. "Religion and Ethnic Ideology: The Hindu Youth Movement in Trinidad." *Ethnic and Racial Studies*, 13 (2): 223–49.

– 1997. "Muslims, the State, and the Public Sphere in Britain." In Gerd Nonneman, Tim Niblock, and Bogdan Szajkowski (eds), *Muslim Communities in the New Europe*. Reading, UK: Ithaca Press.

Waardenburg, J.D.J. 1991. "Muslim Associations and Official Bodies in Some European Countries." In W.A.R. Shadid and P.S. van Koningsveld (eds), *The Integration of Islam and Hinduism in Western Europe*. Kampen, Netherlands: Kok Pharos.

Wallace, Kenyon. 2008. "You Can't Just Sit and Criticize." *Toronto Star*, October 6.

Wang, Jiwu. 2002. "Religious Identity and Ethnic Language: Correlations between Shifting Chinese Canadian Religious Affiliation and Mother Tongue Retention, 1931–1961." *Canadian Ethnic Studies*, 34: 49–74.

Warner, Stephen. 1993. "Toward a New Paradigm for the Sociological Study of Religion in the United States." *American Journal of Sociology*, 98: 1044–93.

Warner, Stephen, and Judith G. Wittner (eds). 1998. *Gathering in Diaspora: Religious Communities and the New Immigration*. Philadelphia: Temple University Press.

Wayland, Sarah V. 1997. "Religious Expression in Public Schools: *Kirpans* in Canada, *Hijab* in France." *Ethnic and Religious Studies*, 20: 545–61.

Weinfeld, Morton. 1981. "Myth and Reality in the Canadian Mosaic: 'Affective Ethncity.'" *Canadian Ethnic Studies*, 13: 80–100.

Weingast, Barry R. 1998. "Constructing Trust: The Political and Economic Roots of Ethnic and Regional Conflict." In Karol Soltan et al. (eds), *Institutions and Social Order*. Ann Arbor: University of Michigan Press.

White, Clinton O. 1994. "Pre-World War I Saskatchewan German Catholic Thought Concerning the Perpetuation of their Language and Religion." *Canadian Ethnic Studies*, 16: 15–45.

Winland, Daphne N. 1992. "The Role of Religious Affiliation in Refugee Resettlement: The Case of the Hmong." *Canadian Ethnic Studies*, 24: 96–120.

Winland, Daphne Naomi. 1993. "The Quest for Mennonite Peoplehood: Ethno-Religious Identity and the Dilemma of Definition." *Canadian Review of Sociology and Anthropology*, 30: 110–12.

Wuthnow, Robert. 1994. *Producing the Sacred. An Essay on Public Religion*. Urbana: University of Illinois Press.

Wuthnow, Robert, and Conrad Hackett. 2003. "The Social Integration of Practitioners of Non-Western Religions in the United States." *Journal for the Scientific Study of Religion*, 42: 651–67.

Yang, Fenggang, and Helen Rose Ebaugh. 2001. "Transformation in New Immigrant Religions and Their Global Implications." *American Sociological Review*, 66: 269–88.

Yousif, Ahmad F. 1993. *Muslims in Canada: A Question of Identity*. Ottawa: Legas.

Zhou, Min, and Carl Bankston. 1998. *Growing Up American*. New York: Russell Sage Foundation.

Znaniecki-Lopata, Helena. 1976. *Polish Americans: Status Competition in an Ethnic Community*. Englewood Cliffs, NJ: Prentice-Hall.

Zolberg, Aristide R., and Long Litt Woon. 1999. "Why Islam is Like Spanish: Cultural Incorporation in Europe and the United States." *Politics and Society*, 27: 5–38.

Index